TWENTIETH-CENTURY POPULISM

TWENTIETH-CENTURY POPULISM

Agricultural Discontent
in the Middle West 1900-1939

E 70

By
THEODORE SALOUTOS
and
JOHN D. HICKS

UNIVERSITY OF NEBRASKA PRESS · Lincoln

*Bison Book edition reprinted from the 1951 edition by arrangement
with the University of Wisconsin Press*

TO

EDWIN BROUN FRED

PRESIDENT OF THE UNIVERSITY OF WISCONSIN
WHOSE INTEREST AND ENCOURAGEMENT
HELPED MAKE THIS BOOK A REALITY

PREFACE

THIS study originated in a series of seminars given by its senior author (Hicks) during the middle 1930's at the University of Wisconsin. At that time, neither the Old Deal nor the New Deal had reached satisfactory solutions for the farmers' ills, and the evidence of discontent was apparent on every hand. Since then the three Triple-A programs and the second World War have changed the situation materially, and the coming of the war has supplied a terminal date for our study. What the future may hold in store for the American farmer is by no means clear, but there is much evidence to support the opinion that neither the Republicans nor the Democrats will risk another Populist revolt by withholding the subsidies that now contribute so heavily to our agricultural income.

The center of agricultural discontent during the first four decades of the twentieth century lay in what we have called the western Middle West, or that part of the Middle West which is bounded on the east by Lake Michigan and the Indiana-Illinois boundary line. But the economic forces that contributed to the farmers' woes had little respect for state boundaries, so that it has seemed better to use in our title the more inclusive term, Middle West. Even that term, if restricted to the twelve north central states, is hardly adequate, but in common parlance the Middle West has come to include all of the central part of the United States, and thus defined, it suits our purpose reasonably well.

A considerable portion of this book was presented by the junior author (Saloutos) as a dissertation for the Ph.D. degree at the University of

Wisconsin in 1940. Since that time, however, the manuscript has been extensively revised and enlarged. As it now stands, Chapters I, II, and IV are primarily the work of Hicks, and the rest of the book the work of Saloutos. But we have consulted and advised together constantly, and we hope that the result is a continuous and unified narrative.

We are deeply indebted to the Committee on Research of the University of Wisconsin for its long-continued support of this project. Professor John D. Black of Harvard University read the manuscript, and favored us with many pertinent suggestions. Finally, we owe much to many libraries and many librarians.

THEODORE SALOUTOS
JOHN D. HICKS

University of California
September 15, 1950

CONTENTS

TWENTIETH-CENTURY POPULISM

Chapter I

THE REGION OF DISCONTENT[1]

I F AMERICANS were obliged to select a heartland for the United States, most of them undoubtedly would point on their maps to the twelve states of the Middle West, or as the census maps have it, the North Central states. Here lie the five states of the old Northwest—Ohio, Indiana, Michigan, Illinois, and Wisconsin—and beyond them in two neatly arranged tiers seven more—Minnesota, Iowa, and Missouri in the first tier and the Dakotas, Nebraska, and Kansas in the second. All of these states are far distant from the seas; they are heavily populated, except on their western and northern fringes, by the most "typical" of Americans; and they are capable of almost unlimited development, both agricultural and industrial. The exploitation of their riches is, indeed, already far along. On one census map after another, throughout the later nineteenth century and into the twentieth, the areas shaded to show acreage under cultivation, or crops harvested, or the production of wheat, or corn, or cattle, or swine, or dairy products reveal clearly the dominant role which this region has played, and continues to play, in the production of food. Here, too, lie the nation's richest deposits of iron ore and some of its richest coal fields. And into this sheltered haven industry also has marched with ever increasing tempo. Probably no other like-sized area could be found in all the world so capable of taking care of all its major needs.

1. This chapter follows in the main an article by John D. Hicks, "The Western Middle West, 1900–1914," *Agricultural History*, XX (April, 1946), pp. 65–77. Reprinted by permission.

It seems clear, however, that a distinction should be made between the eastern and the western Middle West. Exactly where the line of cleavage should be drawn to separate the two might well occasion considerable debate, but most observers would agree that the western Middle West lies wholly to the west of Chicago. One can even mark out a certain geographic unity here. While originally heavily timbered to the north and considerably less so to the south, this territory contains practically all the rich but treeless prairies, land at first spurned by the pioneers but later recognized as ideal for agriculture. Geologists eventually described this great expanse of prairie soils, which widens out westward like a wedge from the northern Indiana-Illinois border, as being among the richest in the world; furthermore, at about the ninety-sixth meridian the prairie soils shaded off into a still richer north-south zone, with a type of soil—the chernozem —so rich that it has been regarded as the ideal against which all others are measured.[2] The breaking plows have done their work, and these great flat or rolling stretches, for hundreds of miles westward from Chicago, offer a minimum of resistance to the farmers' will. On the northern and southern and far western borders of the western Middle West, however, nature has not been quite so kind. In northern Wisconsin and Minnesota the cut-over tracts left by the lumbermen are often sandy and barren. West of the one-hundredth meridian the rainfall is usually inadequate to insure crops without resort to irrigation. Down in southern Missouri the Ozarks have set expansive limits to what the farmer can do. Thus the political and geographic borders of the region do not precisely coincide, but the unity is there nonetheless.

The manner in which most of this western Middle West was opened to settlement offers yet another reason for its separateness. Except for the relatively small areas immediately bordering on the rivers or the lakes, its population grew as its railroad network grew. Most of the eastern Middle West was fairly well settled before the railroads appeared, but in the western Middle West, the exact reverse was true. To be sure, parts of Illinois, southern Wisconsin, eastern and central Missouri, and southeastern Iowa had a considerable population in advance of the railroads, but the era of really rapid settlement set in first during the 1850's as the Illinois Central, the Chicago and North Western, the Chicago and Rock Island, the Bur-

2. Fred A. Shannon, *The Farmers' Last Frontier* (New York, 1945), pp. 12-14.

lington and Missouri River, the Hannibal and St. Joseph, and a host of minor lines began to penetrate where water routes were too far distant for easy use. These and other railroads, helped along in most instances by federal grants of public land turned over to the states for the purpose, built even more feverishly after the Civil War, while great transcontinentals,

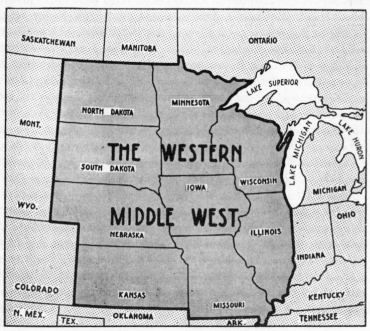

The Center of Agricultural Discontent

aided by land subsidies direct from the United States government, pushed their railheads ever farther and farther west. The western Middle West was thus from its infancy conditioned to railroads. Without them and the markets they opened up, its settlement would have been long delayed and in some portions could hardly have occurred at all.

Another factor tending to emphasize the difference between the eastern and the western Middle West was, and to some extent still is, the degree of industrialization to which each has attained. West of Chicago one finds few really large cities, and agriculture almost everywhere seems dominant. Except for Illinois, where Chicago heavily overweights the scales, as late as the census of 1920, more people in every state of this region still lived in the country, or in the country towns and villages, than in the city.[3] In the older Middle West as in Illinois, the exact reverse was true. If only Chicago and the industrial district surrounding it could be thrown with the eastern Middle West and the rest of Illinois with the western Middle West, the case for the predominantly rural character of the latter region would be complete. Similarly, the eastern Middle West quite outdid the western Middle West in the number and size of its factories. It is true that what is sometimes known as the second mill zone reached as far west as Saint Louis and Minneapolis,[4] but the greater proportion of the region's factories are bracketed by Chicago and Pittsburgh; except for a comparatively few remote outposts, the "black belt" of the manufacturing world leaves off a few miles to the west of Lake Michigan. And, if it makes any difference, a good share of the western outposts of the factory system exist to process foodstuffs or, perchance, to manufacture farm machinery.

There is yet another way in which the western Middle West has established its right to be considered a separate regional entity. Here numerous agrarian movements of reform have been born, here they have lived out their short spans of life, and here they have died. The western Middle West has behind it a long history of agricultural discontent. In the seventies the Grangers, cherishing a grievance against all monopolies in general but against the railroads in particular, captured legislative control of Illinois, Wisconsin, Iowa, and Minnesota and wrote into statute law their doctrine that the states might regulate railroad rates, even to the extent of fixing maximum charges. Following the Grangers came the Greenbackers, whose money reforms attracted followers in every section, but nowhere to quite the extent registered in the western Middle West. In the national election of 1876 Greenback presidential candidates polled over 54 per cent of their popular votes in the states of the western Middle West,

---

3. *Statistical Abstract of the United States,* 1943, p. 12. By 1930 Wisconsin and Missouri had joined Illinois as states with a predominantly urban population, although by very slender majorities.

4. Clifford L. Lord and Elizabeth H. Lord, *Historical Atlas of the United States* (New York, 1944), p. 157.

then only seven in number and not thickly settled at that. Four years later, with many more states offering Greenback tickets, the proportion was still 41 per cent.[5] After the Greenbackers came the Populist revolt. This movement, in its western manifestation, was strongest in the states bordering on the Great Plains—the Dakotas, Nebraska, and Kansas—but it picked up notable followings in both Minnesota and Iowa, and to the latter state it turned in 1892 for a presidential candidate.

In the twentieth century the gusty winds of reform continued to lash the western Middle West. The new crusades rarely struck with equal force in each of the nine states, but there were few periods in which one part or another of the region was not storm-tossed. The Wisconsin Idea got off to a good start early in the century. Hard on its heels came the Iowa Idea. Then, during and after the first World War, the Nonpartisan League upset the equanimity of all "right-thinking" people in North Dakota and Minnesota and to a lesser extent in neighboring states. In Congress the farm bloc, drawing heavily from all the states of the western Middle West, refused to permit the nation to forget the plight of the farmer. Here McNary-Haugenism originated, and here it found its most ardent supporters. Out of the same soil grew also the Farmer-Labor party of Minnesota, the Progressive party of Wisconsin, and many of the agricultural policies of the New Deal. From this region, possibly as a matter of appeasement, came seven of the nine secretaries of agriculture who held office during the first four decades of the twentieth century.

While agricultural discontent, both for the Middle West and for the United States as a whole, centered primarily in this region, economic forces have a way of straying at will across any such interior boundary lines as have been described. The plight of the corn farmer in Ohio and Indiana was not particularly different from the plight of the corn farmer in Illinois and Iowa. Wheat farming in Montana was a kind of projection of wheat farming in North Dakota, and similarly wheat farming in Kansas was much the same as wheat farming in Oklahoma. The Kentucky tobacco grower and the Wisconsin tobacco grower had much in common. Thus any investigation of the sources and consequences of farmer discontent in the western Middle West will frequently involve not only all

5. Based on Edward Stanwood, *A History of the Presidency* (Boston, 1898), pp. 383, 417.

the North Central states, but also, on occasion, some of their near neighbors as well. The term Middle West, however, if interpreted with reasonable elasticity, sets satisfactory limits to the scope of this study.

Obviously, anyone who wishes to understand the agricultural discontent of the Middle West must know something about the way of life that produced it. By 1900 American agriculture was "coming of age"; the era of pioneering was almost over, and each section had begun to realize what it could do best. While "general farming," defined by the census as that in which "no one source of income . . . represents so much as 40 per cent of the total value of products of the farm," was common throughout the Middle West, the tendency lay in the direction of some type of specialized farming particularly suited to the climate, soil, and location of the area concerned.[6] Indeed, the ordinary observer was surprised to discover that, in spite of the fact that nearly every farm grew a considerable variety of crops, there was an unmistakable tendency, region by region, to emphasize one crop above all others. It would overstate the case to compare the farm economy of the Middle West with the one-crop system of the cotton South, but in actual practice one of three principal activities absorbed the chief energies of most of these western farmers. Some of them grew corn, either to sell directly or to feed and sell as livestock; others devoted themselves mainly to the production of wheat; still others raised dairy cattle and made their living by selling milk and butterfat. Thus all three types of farmers, in spite of the numerous minor activities characteristic of most of the better farms, depended for their prosperity upon the marketing of a money crop.

The corn belt cuts a wide swath on any crop map of the United States. Centering in Iowa, all of which it includes, it extends westward into eastern Nebraska and southeastern South Dakota, northward into southern Minnesota, southward into northern Missouri, and eastward across northern and central Illinois on into Indiana and Ohio. In general, the corn farmer had much to be thankful for. He got a larger yield per acre for his labor than any other cereal grower, his crop season was long enough to keep him and his "hands" fully occupied most of the year, he had few problems of storage, and his marketing difficulties were minimum. If he

6. Foster F. Elliott, *Types of Farming in the United States,* U. S. Bureau of the Census (Washington, 1933), p. 48.

sold his corn directly, he found plenty of nearby purchasers who were ready to take it off his hands in order to feed it to livestock. Less than 20 per cent of the corn crop was shipped beyond the borders of the county in which it was raised. If he himself fed cattle or hogs, he was able to "condense" his freights. Ninety per cent of the corn crop, according to a common view, should never leave the farm on which it is grown. Every steer could conveniently carry a hundred bushels of corn to market, and in the thirty months of its normal life expectancy, it should consume also two or three acres of grass.[7] Livestock growers could always find plenty to complain about, but the packing houses to which they shipped were relatively close at hand, and in spite of the toll taken by the railroads and the commission men, profits were reasonably good.

Wheat was produced in many parts of the United States, but the greatest concentration of wheat growing was found in two large areas of the western Middle West. What came to be known as the hard spring wheat belt centered in North Dakota, but with a formidable extension in every direction—eastward into Minnesota, southward into South Dakota, westward into Montana, and northwest across the American border into the Canadian Northwest. Well to the south of this region lay another wheat-growing area, now commonly called the hard winter wheat belt, with Kansas as the center and overflowing into Nebraska, Colorado, western Oklahoma, and northern Texas. The growing of wheat had been a favorite frontier occupation, particularly after the thrust of population from the east reached the open prairies. Wheat is a highly concentrated crop, "storable," "haulable," and "salable" even under pioneer conditions. Furthermore, wheat culture thrives best on land plentifully supplied with humus, a condition present in most of the prairie states when the sod was first broken. There, too, the use of large-scale harvesting and threshing machinery was practicable. Pioneer farmers usually grew wheat as long as the soil produced a paying crop, then either moved westward to new prairie lands or gave up wheat growing for other and more complicated types of agriculture.[8]

As the twentieth century opened, the semiarid High Plains were begin-

7. *Wallaces' Farmer*, XXXVIII (February 21, 1913), p. 314.
8. Elliott, *Types of Farming*, p. 26; *Wallaces' Farmer*, XXXIII (October 2, 1908), p. 1179.

ning to set boundaries to the westward march of wheat. But a notable discovery had been made. Given modern milling conditions, the best bread wheats were not the soft wheats long favored by eastern farmers and millers but the hard wheats of high gluten content that could be produced only in regions of limited rainfall. This discovery, together with the introduction and improvement of turkey red, a variety of Russian hard winter wheat, had much to do with the rapid expansion of the hard winter wheat belt into western Kansas, the Oklahoma Panhandle, and northern Texas. As time went on, it became customary in the manufacture of bread flour either to use the hard wheats exclusively or to mix them with the soft winter wheats grown in Missouri, Illinois, and many eastern states. In times of shortage in the American hard wheat crop, millers sometimes felt obliged to import Canadian hard wheat, despite the tariff.[9]

There was a considerable difference in the methods by which spring wheat and winter wheat were produced. The spring wheat grower sowed his grain as early in the spring as he could and then harvested his crop from 100 to 110 days later. Winter wheat was sown in September or October and harvested the following June or July, thus requiring a ten-month season. In general, the winter wheat growers tended to be better farmers than the spring wheat growers, but the short work year was common to both. Conceivably, as one writer has put it, the wheat farmer could "put in a crop during a two- or three-week period in the fall or spring and harvest it in a like period during the summer or autumn; leaving at least ten months of the year free for vacation or other pursuits."[10]

The third principal type of economy upon which farmers of the western Middle West came to depend was the dairy industry. The rapid expansion of dairy farming was due principally to the demand of the great new urban centers for milk. Indeed, the new city population meant not only new milk customers, but as time went on it meant also more milk per customer. Educational campaigns changed the food habits of city dwellers and in particular taught them the virtues of the "perfect food," milk.

9. James C. Malin, *Winter Wheat in the Golden Belt of Kansas* (Lawrence, Kans., 1944), pp. 188–209, 254.

10. Edwin G. Nourse and Others, *America's Capacity to Produce* (Washington, 1934), p. 39; Theodore Saloutos, "Farmer Movements since 1902" (unpublished doctoral dissertation, University of Wisconsin, 1940), p. 3.

So great was the demand that means of transportation were devised to tap the milk supply a hundred, two hundred, or even three hundred miles from the city markets. In addition to milk for direct consumption, dairy farmers also sold butterfat to local creameries and comparatively small quantities of milk to ice cream makers, cheese factories, and condenseries. The production of butter and cheese began far back in the nineteenth century and antedated the urban era, but as with other food items, the increase in the number of city consumers greatly increased the demand.[11]

While cities inevitably furnished the principal market for milk, proximity to urban centers turned out to be only one factor in determining the location of dairy farms. The condition of the land mattered far less to the dairy farmer than to the grain grower, for a well-managed dairy farm tended to build up the soil rather than to deplete it. Naturally, therefore, where wheat growing or other types of general farming had robbed the soil of its fertility, dairy farming furnished a reasonable alternative. Rough and worn-out fields could be turned to pasture, and dairy farming produced an ample supply of fertilizer with which to stimulate the growth of feed crops. But the successful dairy farmer had to be a good farmer, intelligent as well as industrious and able to keep abreast of the rapid progress that scientific agriculture was making in his specialty.

The greatest concentration of dairy farming in the Middle West was in Wisconsin, northern Illinois, northwestern Iowa, and central and eastern Minnesota. Nearby lay the markets of Chicago, Milwaukee, St. Paul, Minneapolis, and numerous lesser cities. The urban influence, however, was less important in determining the location of dairy farms engaged principally in the production of butterfat. For this purpose some of the heaviest areas of concentration lay at a considerable distance from the large cities. There was, indeed, a considerable amount of dairy farming throughout the entire corn belt and even in the remoter grain-growing areas. It is also worth noting that the farmers of Wisconsin produced the milk that made that state for many decades the chief center of cheese manufacturing in the nation.[12]

11. Henry E. Alvord, "Dairy Development in the United States," U. S. Dept. Agri., *Yearbook*, 1899, pp. 381–402. See also *Wallaces' Farmer*, XXXIII (October 16, 1908), p. 1251.   12. Elliott, *Types of Farming*, pp. 44, 54.

The dairy farmer enjoyed certain substantial advantages over the grain grower. His work was less seasonal than that of any other farmer and provided employment for himself, his family, and his employees the whole year around. His profits, likewise, were fairly evenly distributed throughout the year, instead of coming in only at crop-marketing time. He had less to fear from high transportation charges, for his products were of small bulk in comparison to their value, and freight rates loomed correspondingly less important. His investment in land was moderate, and the stability of conditions under which he operated tended to make his credit good. What he asked of government was mainly low taxes, protection against substitutes, and aid in the never ending search for greater production at lower cost.[13]

It must not be forgotten that on most farms, whether in the corn belt, or in one of the chief wheat-growing regions, or in the area chiefly devoted to the dairy industry, there was generally a considerable amount of mixed farming. In the Middle West almost all varieties of cereal crops such as oats, barley, rye, and buckwheat were grown successfully. Milk and butterfat came from the same farms that also marketed swine and beef cattle. Fruits and vegetables were raised everywhere for domestic consumption and on a few truck farms for market. Potatoes were an important specialty in limited areas of Minnesota, Wisconsin, and Missouri. Sugar beets were raised in parts of Nebraska, tobacco growing achieved some importance in Wisconsin, and chickens, turkeys, geese, and ducks were universal. But in spite of these many side issues, the most important activities of farmers in the western Middle West centered on corn or corn and livestock, on wheat, and on dairy farming.[14]

Another circumstance, clearly apparent to the most casual observer, was the prevalence of the single-family farm. There were exceptions, of course, but in general the farmer of this region lived on his own or on rented land and carried on his farming activities mainly with such aid as he could obtain from his wife and children. The larger his crop of boys and girls

13. Benton H. Wilcox, "A Reconsideration of the Character and Economic Basis of Northwestern Radicalism" (unpublished doctoral dissertation, University of Wisconsin, 1933), pp. 33, 56.

14. See the appended map showing type-of-farming areas in 1930 in Elliott, *Types of Farming*.

old enough to help with the work, the better he was able to handle his labor problem. If he needed more help than his own family could give him, the hired man or hired hand, most probably the grown son of some other farmer, was introduced to supplement the family labor supply. If the farmer's wife, with the help of her own daughters, could not do all the work that fell to her lot, she sought the aid of a hired girl. Neither the hired man nor the hired girl was thought of as an inferior; in many instances the hired man became a son-in-law, and the hired girl a daughter-in-law. Working out as a hired man was a generally accepted method by which any young man without means obtained the start necessary to begin farming on his own.[15]

The ideal size of a family farm was traditionally 160 acres, and on the average the actual was not far from the ideal. This was the size of the farm allowed to each settler under the terms of the Homestead Act of 1862, but most of the farms in the Middle West had never been homesteads. The Homestead Act allotted 160 acres to each settler merely because a farm of that size had long been considered to be about right for one individual to operate. Eighty-acre farms were regarded as too small for economical farming: they required the same outlay for housing, work horses, and machinery as the larger farm but produced only half as much; they furnished more work than the farmer could do alone but not enough to justify his employing a year-round farm hand; and in the corn belt, where thrifty farmers expected about 90 per cent of their land to be tillable, the corn rows were likely to be too short.[16]

Farming was definitely a capitalistic affair and required a heavy investment. The size of the investment depended mainly upon the price of land, which varied from place to place and from time to time. A typical northwestern farm, according to one estimate, in 1910 would have represented an investment of $12,000. Of this sum about $1,400 would have been in buildings, $350 in machinery, and $1,400 in livestock—the rest, of course, in land.[17] Not every farm, by any means, was wholly free from mortgage, while in many cases chattel loans and store bills added ma-

15. Paul S. Taylor, "The American Hired Man: His Rise and Decline," U. S. Bureau of Agricultural Economics, *Land Policy Review,* VI (Spring, 1943), pp. 3–17.

16. *Wallaces' Farmer,* XXXIX (March 27, 1914), p. 540.

17. Wilcox, "Northwestern Radicalism," p. 23.

terially to the farmer's burden of debt. But the farm loan or farm mortgage was not necessarily an evidence of thriftlessness. It might, on the contrary, be regarded as a kind of evidence of prosperity. The wise farmer improved his buildings, bought new machinery, or expanded his acres even if to do so meant borrowing the necessary funds. Credit for the farmer was as necessary and proper as credit for any other businessman.

A burning problem throughout the entire Middle West was the steady increase in farm tenancy. "Nothing is more important to this country," said Theodore Roosevelt in 1907, "than the perpetuation of our system of medium sized farms worked by their owners. We do not want to see our farmers sink to the condition of the peasants in the old world, barely able to live on their small holdings, nor do we want to see their places taken by wealthy men owning enormous estates which they work purely by tenants and hired servants."[18] And yet, it seemed evident that something akin to the condition Roosevelt feared was coming about. Census statistics showed a steady increase in tenancy throughout the Middle West, and even more alarming, an increase which made tenancy more marked in this region than anywhere else in the United States except the South. In Iowa, for example, 76.2 per cent of the farms had been owned by their occupants in 1880, but thirty years later, in 1910, only 62.2 per cent were so owned. Furthermore, only half the farms of the state were operated exclusively by their owners.[19] Four years later, on the eve of the first World War, according to a reliable authority, almost 40 per cent of the farms in the corn belt were being cultivated by tenants. In parts of Illinois this proportion was no doubt well above 50 per cent, while in some of the newer and more sparsely settled sections it dropped to less than 20 per cent. But the long-cherished ideal, according to which each farmer owned his own farm and was thus accountable to himself alone, seemed farther from reality each succeeding year. If the tenant farmers were only organized, wrote one realistic observer, they could easily control elections and take over the state governments.[20]

18. *Wallaces' Farmer*, XXXII (October 11, 1907), p. 1145. On this subject in general, see W. J. Spillman and E. A. Goldenweiser, "Farm Tenantry in the United States," U. S. Dept. Agri., *Yearbook*, 1916, pp. 321–46.

19. *Thirteenth Census of the United States*, 1910, Vol. VI, *Agriculture*, p. 507.

20. *Wallaces' Farmer*, XXXV (November 4, 1910), p. 1494; XXXVII (March 8, 1912), p. 455; (June 28, 1912), p. 1019; XXXIX (March 27, 1914), p. 541.

There were two principal types of landlords. One was the retired farmer who, at perhaps sixty years of age, gave up farming and moved to town. Sometimes he rented to a son or son-in-law or nephew, and thus to a prospective heir, but in most cases he counted on enough from rent to take care of his needs. Thousands of these retired farmers had begun life as farm hands and had then become tenants, then farm owners, and at last retired farmers able to live on their rents and the interest on their savings. Many of them continued to take an active interest—frequently too active an interest for the tenant's peace of mind—in the farms they had left. Retired farmers often found that they had underestimated the expense of living in town and were inspired to drive new and harder bargains with their tenants, while in their communities they became "stationary" citizens, men who could be counted upon to vote consistently against better schools or city improvements on the sole ground that anything that might raise taxes was wrong.[21]

Another type of landlord was the investor, or as he was more likely to be called, the speculator. Farm land in the Middle West had for many years risen steadily in value and was thus considered by many investors to be safer than any bond, mortgage, or security on the market. Counting in the prospective rise in value of the farm, landownership seemed to promise a higher rate of return than any comparable investment. Investment-minded landlords, unlike the retired farmer, might know nothing whatever of farming, and some of them were totally unconscious of the need of keeping up the fertility of the land they owned. The worst of them seemed to "regard the farm as something like the old-fashioned coupon bond, from which they can clip coupons twice a year on the particular day and date on which they are due, whether crops are good or bad."[22]

While some farms fell to landlord-investors through the foreclosure of mortgages, there was another quite different cause of landlordism. Many prosperous farmers, convinced that land values had reached too high a figure, sold out their farms and moved north, west, or south to newer and

21. *Report of the Country Life Commission* (60 Congress, 2 session, Senate Document 705, serial 5408, Washington, 1909), p. 21.

22. *Wallaces' Farmer*, XXXIV (January 8, 1909), p. 40. See also E. H. Thomson and H. M. Dixon, *A Farm-Management Survey of Three Representative Areas in Indiana, Illinois, and Iowa*, U. S. Dept. Agri., Bulletin 41 (Washington, 1914).

cheaper lands. The number of Americans, mostly farmers, who left the United States for Canada exceeded 100,000 annually by 1911, while other thousands moved to the Mountain States, to the Pacific Coast, to the South, and even to Mexico.[23] These migrations were attended by far greater risks than most of the migrating farmers fully understood. Farming by irrigation or farming in an area of reduced rainfall involved new techniques, and while the land was cheaper, the man who purchased it was often poorer before he mastered them. Corn belt farmers who went west found out, usually only by experience, that beyond the ninety-ninth meridian conditions of corn growing were far less satisfactory than in the regions from which they had come. But they left in numbers just the same, and upon the land they vacated there often came tenants who were far less able to do the work than the men who had sold out. The time had come, said one editorialist, when Americans should settle down. "The farmers of the United States have been playing leapfrog over each other for over a hundred years, in fact, ever since the Revolution. . . . It is time for us to realize that the value of land depends more than anything else on the men who farm it."[24] But, at least as far as Iowa was concerned, all such pleas were in vain. That state lost steadily in farm population, and the census of 1910 even showed a decline in the total number of inhabitants.[25]

Rents paid by tenants varied. The prevailing rent in Illinois, according to one landlord, was half the corn, two-fifths the oats, and $5 an acre for meadow and pasture. In the corn belt states generally it was customary for the tenant to pay from one-third to one-half the grain he raised as rent. He was required, as a rule, to furnish all the necessary teams, implements, and seed, and in addition whatever labor was necessary to cultivate the land and keep it in good shape. He might also be expected to pay the

---

23. Senate Document 705, 60 Congress, 2 session, p. 49.

24. *Wallaces' Farmer*, XXXVIII (October 31, 1913), p. 1475. See also *ibid.*, XXXIX (July 24, 1914), p. 1044:

> "I never saw an oft removed tree,
> Nor yet an oft removed familee,
> That throve so well
> As one that settled be."

25. *Thirteenth Census of the United States*, 1910, *Abstract*, p. 24.

cost of threshing and to deliver the grain to the elevator free of charge. Owners who furnished teams or other equipment for their tenants took a correspondingly larger share of the crop. Cash rentals, which were very common, ranged from $2 to $5 or $6 an acre, depending upon the productiveness of the land. Sometimes land on which crops were raised was rented for a share of the crop, while meadow or pasture land on the same farm was rented at so much per acre. Cash tenants complained bitterly that their rents were raised much more rapidly than the rise in price of farm products justified and that they were certain to get a raise in rent if they exerted themselves to build up a farm in order to make it pay.[26]

While some landlords were benevolent and thoughtful, others cared little for their tenants' welfare. Most landlords insisted on a short-term lease, usually good for only one year. The tenants, landlords held, were an inferior lot as a whole and not to be trusted. The only way an owner could protect his farm was to be able to get rid of a poor tenant in the briefest possible time. The one-year tenant, however, condemned to uncertainty of tenure and to frequent moving, tried to get all he could out of the land while he was on it and to give to it the least possible attention in return. Rented farms were often distinguished by their poorly kept buildings, their deepening gullies, and their infertile acres. Landlords were frequently short-sighted along other lines also. They objected to making the improvements necessary to enable their tenants to farm at a profit. Or, if they consented grudgingly to erect buildings and fences and to lay tile for drainage, they might require the tenant to board the carpenters and other workmen free of charge, not to mention hauling in the needed materials and filling up the ditches after the tile had been laid.[27]

In quality the tenant farmers varied widely. In spite of the handicaps under which they labored, many of them were in reality good farmers. Some had once been farm laborers and by saving their wages had accumulated enough capital to start in as tenant farmers. Such persons expected to emerge eventually as farm owners and in many instances did so. A few had fallen in the economic scale, whether from bad luck or bad farming or bad management, and had become tenants where once they

26. *Wallaces' Farmer,* XXXIII (November 13, 1908), p. 1388; XXXV (September 9, 1910), p. 1184.
27. *Ibid.,* XXXIII (December 18, 1908), p. 1582.

had been owners. For many the climb from tenancy to farm ownership was a difficult, if not impossible, task to perform.[28]

The relationship between high tenancy and high land values was striking. According to the census of 1910 this parallelism was evident in two-thirds of the states in the Middle West. High-priced land that was held for speculative purposes was always for rent, and in these states there usually were tenants to take a good deal of it. By contrast, in the newer parts of Minnesota, North Dakota, and South Dakota, where there was land "begging for occupants," it had to be worked by the owner or not at all. The low tenancy rate in these parts held down the general average for those states, in spite of the speculation and tenancy in the older sections. This relationship between the value of land and tenancy was also found to exist in certain groups of counties within such a state, for example, as Illinois.

Likewise, there was a close tie between tenancy and the types of farming engaged in. According to the census of 1900 the tenant farmers of the Middle West had supervision of more than their proportional number of farms on which hay and grain were the principal products and a little more than half their proportion of the livestock farms. The tenants raised grain to sell, while the landowners usually raised it to feed to their livestock; they produced only three-fourths of their proportional share of hay and forage, and were even further behind the landowning farmers in the ownership of sheep. As for hogs, the tenants raised their full number. They grew only two-thirds of their share of wheat and exceeded by one-third their proportional share of corn. In some of the wheat-growing states, however, the tenants raised more than their share. With respect to corn, conditions were more nearly uniform throughout, although the tenants raised proportionately more than did the landowners. Vegetables, fruit, and tobacco usually were grown by the landowning farmers.

The character of the tenant farm itself was of some importance. The value of the farm per acre was about the same, but the buildings were

28. Senate Document 705, 60 Congress, 2 session, pp. 41–42; *Wallaces' Farmer*, XXXIV (January 1, 1909), p. 4; *Report of the Special Committee on Farm Tenancy* (75 Congress, 1 session, House Document 149, serial 10126, Washington, 1937). The validity of the "agricultural ladder hypothesis" is strongly attacked by L. F. Cox, "Tenancy in the United States," *Agricultural History*, XVIII (July, 1944), pp. 97–105.

likely to be worth about five-sixths as much as those on the farm occupied by its owner. The tenant had a little less than his proportional
share of implements and farm machinery, in part because his need was
less for such items as haying tools, corn binders, or milk separators.
Hibbard pictured the tenant farmer in 1910 as one who was much younger
than the landowner and as one who stayed on the same farm about a
third as long. He was likely to have poor buildings and comparatively little grassland and livestock, and probably would be devoting his time to the
raising of grain to haul to market, although he might feed much of his
corn to hogs.

These conditions seem to indicate that the high price of land was not
the sole reason for "the concentration of tenancy on the better land." The
tenant farmer usually lacked the capital and was ill equipped to raise
stock on a wider basis. He wanted returns that same year and not several
years later. Usually the landlord gave him no encouragement to raise livestock because that would require a great deal of money to build the necessary barns, silos, and fences. Even if the farmer wanted to raise stock, he
was likely to be discouraged by the fact that he would probably have to
move soon. All this seemed to indicate that the tenant veered toward that
type of farming for which he felt best fitted and which best met his needs.
The one thing upon which the landlord and tenant were completely
agreed was that they both wanted "prompt returns on the outlay."[29]

Critics of the farm tenancy system pointed out that the first and most
important reform was to get rid of the one-year lease. They urged that the
tenant be assured tenure as long as he farmed satisfactorily and also im-
munity from frequent and unreasonable increases in rent. The English
system, which conceded the right of the tenant to whatever fertility he
had put into the soil without being able to harvest it, was cited as an example for American landlords. In England, unlike the situation in the
United States, a tenant could count on a virtually permanent lease and
just treatment. Should the landlord grow careless with the tenant's rights,
the tenant had the right of action at law for damages.[30]

29. B. H. Hibbard, "Tenancy in the North Central States," in T. N. Carver, ed.,
Selected Readings in Rural Economics (Boston, 1916), pp. 511–22.
30. *Wallaces' Farmer*, XXXVIII (April 11, 1913), p. 650; (October 10, 1913),
p. 1372.

Granted that farm tenancy had undesirable social consequences, the soil depletion practices that prevailed throughout the nineteenth century can hardly be chalked up to tenancy alone. Farm owners as well as tenants were responsible for this. The extensive, as opposed to the intensive, type of farming that was practiced encouraged a "mining" of the soil, and the resulting exhaustion helped to bring down the yield per acre. "This lessening of soil fertility," declared the Country Life Commission appointed by President Roosevelt in 1908, "is marked in every part of the United States, even in the richest lands of the prairies. It marks the pioneer stage of land usage. It has now become an acute national danger, and the economic, social, and political problems arising out of it must at once receive the best attention of statesmen."[31]

And yet American agriculture in the first decade of the twentieth century, particularly in the Middle West, gave the appearance of great prosperity. "The value of the farm products," wrote Secretary of Agriculture James Wilson in his annual report for the year 1909, "is so incomprehensibly large that it has become merely a row of figures."[32] "There has never been a time," declared the Country Life Commission, "when the American farmer was as well off as he is to-day, when we consider not only his earning power, but the comforts and advantages he may secure."[33] According to another observer, "One American harvest would buy the kingdom of Belgium, king and all; two would buy Italy; three would buy Austria-Hungary; and five, at a spot-cash price, would take Russia from the czar."[34] In short, the farmers, tenants and landlords alike, were making money. Farm labor was fully employed and at what, for the times, were considered high wages. Prosperity showed itself in the improved character of farm homes, often surrounded by attractive lawns and gardens, in the multiplication of better barns and farm buildings, in the sanitary water supplies and plumbing equipment that farmers were beginning to enjoy, in the increasing availability of good reading matter on farm tables, and in the farmers' demand for better educational facilities

31. *Ibid.*, XXXIII (September 4, 1908), p. 1061; Senate Document 705, 60 Congress, 2 session, pp. 38, 41.

32. U. S. Dept. Agri., *Yearbook*, 1909, p. 9.

33. Senate Document 705, 60 Congress, 2 session, p. 21.

34. H. N. Casson, in *Wallaces' Farmer*, XXXIII (July 10, 1908), p. 871.

for their sons and daughters.[35] The case of the man who went through "the worst" in Kansas during the nineteenth century, but had become one of the stockholders and directors in the local bank, owned an automobile, and sent his children to college before the twentieth was far along was only one among many.

The prosperity of the American farmer during the early years of the twentieth century was due in large part to the high prices he was able to command for the commodities he had to sell. The Secretary of Agriculture, in his report for 1910, pointed out that if the year 1899 were regarded as 100, the value of farm products had risen as follows: 1900, 106.4; 1905, 133; 1907, 158.7; 1908, 167.3; 1909, 182.8; and 1910, 189.2.[36] Under these circumstances it seemed reasonable to assume that there was "good money for every man on good land who farms right." After 1910, the steady rise in farm prices was somewhat arrested, but compared to the low quotations of the nineties the farmers' receipts seemed excellent indeed. Wheat in 1914 brought around 80 cents a bushel, corn from 60 to 70 cents a bushel, butter from 25 to 30 cents a pound, and other farm prices in proportion. Such prices contrasted markedly with those of the nineties, when wheat sold for from 50 to 60 cents, corn for 25 to 30 cents, and butter from 12 to 20 cents.[37]

Attempts to explain the prevailing high prices were widely varied. Some, President Taft for example, held that the trouble was merely an increase in consumption without a corresponding increase in production, or as another phrased it, "Population has simply been increasing more rapidly than farm products; too many people in the town—too few on the farm."[38] Others noted that any greatly increased production seemed unlikely in the future, since practically the entire public domain had already been absorbed, while lands in the older sections were rapidly losing their fertility. The expansion of the corn belt seemed particularly improbable,

35. Senate Document 705, 60 Congress, 2 session, p. 20; *Wallaces' Farmer,* XXXIV (January 8, 1909), p. 40.

36. U. S. Dept. Agri., *Yearbook,* 1910, p. 10.

37. *Ibid.,* 1914, pp. 517, 529, 624; *Wallaces' Farmer,* XXXV (May 6, 1910), p. 745; (December 23, 1910), p. 1734.

38. Myron T. Herrick, *Preliminary Report on Land and Agricultural Credit in Europe* (62 Congress, 3 session, Senate Document 967, serial 6364, Washington, 1912–13), p. 5; *Wallaces' Farmer,* XXXVI (March 24, 1911), p. 542.

for the growing of corn, due to climatic reasons, was confined to an area already fully exploited. Furthermore, important new uses were being found for corn. Careful observers noted that the rising level of prices was by no means confined to the United States alone, and some of them argued that the increase in the world's supply of gold was partly responsible for price trends. The real trouble, they said, was that gold inflation had resulted in a steady decline in the purchasing power of the dollar.[39]

The high farm prices were deeply resented by the consumer public. Sometimes farmers were denounced as conscienceless monopolists who set the prices of the necessities of life to the disadvantage of every city dweller. Manufacturers claimed that the American farmer was lazy and inefficient. If only he would get busy and increase production, food would be cheaper, the wages of city laborers could be lowered, and the American manufacturer could the better meet foreign competition. But the farmers were disturbed only by the fear that the good prices might not last. Senator Porter J. McCumber of North Dakota voiced their sentiments when he said:

We are now approaching a condition when the farmer is about to secure equality of remuneration, and the moment we reach toward that goal of justice a boycott is started against his products, both in the cities and in the National Legislature, by the introduction of bills designed to destroy his profits. . . . He is, however, receiving not one cent more for any article than he is justly entitled to, and in my candid opinion he is not receiving as much to-day as he is going to receive in the future, and in the very near future.[40]

But high prices for farm produce did not wholly explain the prosperity of the American farmer during the early years of the twentieth century. He was aided also by a phenomenal rise in the price of land. For the country as a whole, according to the census of 1910, land values increased during the preceding decade by 118.1 per cent. In states like Wisconsin and Minnesota, with a large proportion of cut-over timber land, the increase was less than this, but as the following percentages show, the advance was

39. *Ibid.*, XXXIV (October 1, 1909), p. 1219; XXXV (November 25, 1910), p. 1570; XXXVII (September 6, 1912), p. 1242.

40. *Congressional Record,* 61 Congress, 2 session, Vol. 45, Part II (1910), pp. 1479-80; *Wallaces' Farmer,* XXXV (March 11, 1910), pp. 431-32. See also *ibid.* (April 22, 1910), p. 679.

far greater in some of the states of the western Middle West: Wisconsin, 71.9; Minnesota, 82.2; Illinois, 104.1; Missouri, 107.9; Iowa, 123.0; Kansas, 189.0; Nebraska, 231.8; North Dakota, 321.3; and South Dakota, 377.1.[41] Numerous records of land sales backed up the census figures. Iowa lands that sold at from $10 to $30 an acre thirty years before were selling in 1908 at from $80 to $125. Lands six miles distant from a railroad that were worth only $3 to $5 an acre in the 1870's, and from $25 to $30 an acre in the 1880's, brought from $135 to $155 an acre in 1910. Farmers who had been able to hold onto their farms had thus accumulated wealth at a rapid rate, not so much from the prices for which farm products sold as from the rapidly appreciating value of the acres they owned. Mortgages that had occasioned the greatest anxiety a few years earlier could now be regarded as negligible. Whether he realized it or not, the average middle western landowner had made his money not so much from good farming as from the unearned increment that came with the ownership of farm lands. To a considerable extent, he was only a successful speculator.[42]

Explanations for the rise in land values were as varied as those which were advanced to explain the rising prices paid for farm products. Higher prices for grain, livestock, and dairy produce would of course tend naturally to boost land prices, but the increase in value of farm lands had quite outrun the increase in price of farm products. Nor could the rising price of land be ascribed to its increased productivity, for in spite of the best efforts of the proponents of scientific agriculture, the yield per acre had risen at best only a very little. Much was made of the supposed "disappearance of free land" on the theory that the supply of available land was being cut down just when the demand for it was greatest. Actually, there was much free land then available in the arid west, and a good deal of it was being taken up by homesteaders.[43] But lands that required expensive irrigation works to make them productive were hardly "free," while unirrigated lands were a bad gamble for most pioneers. Probably the demand for land really was up and the supply of good land down. Farms

41. *Thirteenth Census of the United States*, 1910, Vol. V, *Agriculture*, pp. 28, 79, and plate facing p. 44; Senate Document 705, 60 Congress, 2 session, p. 20.

42. *Wallaces' Farmer* XXXIII (September 4, 1908), p. 1061; XXXIV (December 31, 1909), p. 1704; XXXV (March 4, 1910), p. 369.

43. Fred A. Shannon, "The Homestead Act and the Labor Surplus," *American Historical Review*, XLI (July, 1936), pp. 637-51.

were worth more also because of the improvements their owners had made on them, the greater availability of markets, and the better roads and schools which they had paid for, and because of the world's increasing gold supply, which had inflated all prices. Undoubtedly, also, the speculative spirit was influential. Farmers, instead of depositing their savings in banks or investing in industrial stocks and bonds, bought more lands, knowing that land values were sure to rise. Speculators who had no interest whatever in farming bought land for the 6 or 8 per cent annual rise in value that seemed a certainty throughout the early years of the century.[44]

This picture of high prices and general agricultural prosperity contrasted oddly with the fact that farm population relatively, and in many communities actually, was on the decline. As already noted, the state of Iowa, one of the richest in the corn belt and one almost exclusively dependent on agriculture, showed an actual loss, a loss which amounted to .3 per cent in the population of the state as a whole during the years 1900–10. But in this state, as in many others, the most notable fact was the drift of the people from the farms to the towns and cities. Wherever the land was most valuable for agricultural purposes, it seemed that the decline in country population was most marked. Cities everywhere had grown. Iowa, in spite of its decrease in population, found that its principal city, Des Moines, had an increase of 39 per cent during the very decade when the population of the state as a whole was falling off.[45]

Several factors entered into the explanation of this exodus from the farms of the Middle West. Of fundamental importance was the increasing reliance upon agricultural machinery. With the new machines, fewer farmers could produce more goods. "A boy with four horses and a modern

44. Senate Document 705, 60 Congress, 2 session, pp. 20, 30, 40; *Wallaces' Farmer* XXXVI (September 15, 1911), p. 1260; XXXVII (December 6, 1912), p. 1716.

An interesting formula has been worked out for the estimation of land values. To obtain the present value (PV) of a farm, divide the expected annual increase (a) by the expected rate of interest (r). Thus $PV = a/r$. If, however, the income of the farm is expected to increase, then the value of the farm will also increase. To measure this increase in land value for a given year, add to the present value the expected annual increase (i) divided by r^2. Thus $V = a/r + i/r^2$. John D. Black and Others, *Farm Management* (New York, 1947), pp. 737-38.

45. *Thirteenth Census of the United States, 1910, Abstract*, p. 68. See also *Wallaces' Farmer*, XXXV (November 4, 1910), p. 1493; (November 18, 1910), p. 1540; XXXIX (May 29, 1914), p. 851.

binder can cut and bind as much in one day as from ten to fifteen men could in a day in the time of his grandfather." But some blame lay also with the high prices that lands in the Middle West had begun to command. It was because of these prices that so many farmers sold out to their neighbors or to speculators and invested in farms located in newer areas where the prices were not so high. This movement of population did not lessen the nation's total farm population, but it did lessen the number of farmers in regions where land prices were excessively high. Most discussed of all the causes of rural decline was the lure of the city. Farm boys and girls were attracted by the higher wages and shorter hours that went with city jobs. They craved the excitement of city life, the superior comfort of city homes, and the variety of opportunities that the cities offered.[46]

It was this competition with the city that made the problem of farm labor so persistently acute. Farm labor, as those who really knew patiently explained, was skilled labor. A boy who had grown up on a farm knew many things that only years of experience could teach. When he left to work on the railroads, or in the factories, or in city stores, the loss to the farm was serious. Farm labor actually commanded very high wages, enough sometimes to enable the thrifty farm laborer to save from $200 to $250 per year. But so much of his pay came in board, shelter, heat, and washing and ironing that it was hard to make the farm boy see that the $20 and up he could earn on the farm was nearly all clear profit and not to be compared with the city wages from which he must pay high prices for board and room and for every service. Efforts to turn the tide of immigration farmward were not very helpful. The European immigrant, even if he had been a peasant, knew little of American farming methods and was practically useless on the typical American farm. Furthermore, he too liked the city better and generally preferred to stay there. As for unemployed city workers, they were apt to be a positive liability. If only an adequate supply of farm labor could be obtained, some said, crops could readily be increased by 25 per cent. "The greatest problem of the statesman of the future is to keep enough men on the land to make it produce the food required at prices the consumer can afford to pay."[47]

46. *Ibid.*, XXXIV (January 8, 1909), p. 43; XXXV (November 4, 1910), pp. 1467, 1493.
47. Senate Document 705, 60 Congress, 2 session, p. 42. See also *Wallaces' Farmer,*

The decline in rural population was a source of considerable worry to farm and city residents alike. Thoughtful observers sought long and earnestly for a remedy. Something must be done, they concluded, to improve "social conditions in the open country." The thesis almost universally accepted was that if the schools, churches, roads, home conveniences, and social activities of the farm could only be made to equal those of the city, there would be no further serious lack of people on the farm. The rural free delivery of mail and the party telephone line helped some but hardly enough to overcome the "isolation and utter barrenness" of country life. The need for good roads seemed obvious, but many landowners, fearful lest they have to foot the gigantic tax bill involved, were strangely skeptical. Besides, if the roads were improved, wouldn't the farmers use them mainly to go to town? What could be done to renovate the country church and make it a more satisfying social center? What could be done to promote the formation of social organizations comparable to the once active but now almost forgotten Grange? What could be done to provide sports and amusements in the country comparable with those so readily available in the city? Until answers for such questions as these could be found, it was idle to preach the gospel of back-to-the-farm. The matter of first importance was to keep the people on the farm who were already there.[48]

The status of the rural town was hardly better than that of the open country. Such local manufacturing activities as flour milling, wagon making, general blacksmithing, and tanning had once made each town a little industrial center. But establishments of larger capital, located at strategic points, had put most of the local manufacturers out of business. Even as merchandising centers the towns were running down. Sales direct to the farm from the factory or from mail-order houses cut in seriously on the profits of the small-town merchant. Retired farmers, with their chronic fear of taxes, kept civic improvements at a minimum. Boys and girls from the towns, no less than those from the farms, were hypnotized by the good wages and the bright lights of the city. The time had been

XXXIV (November 12, 1909), p. 1451; XXXV (February 11, 1910), p. 219; XXXV (February 10, 1911), p. 214; XXXIX (July 3, 1914), p. 973.

48. Senate Document 705, 60 Congress, 2 session, p. 14; *Wallaces' Farmer* XXXIV (October 22, 1909), p. 1338; XXXV (January 7, 1910), p. 2.

when the country town fronted toward the farm and was principally identified with rural life; now the town fronted rather toward the city, imitated the city, and, as fast as it could manage, moved to the city.[49]

What most concerned the public at large about the farm problem was the fear, duly re-enforced by the rising price of foodstuffs, that agricultural production would be unable to keep pace with the growth of the nation. The population of the United States had increased from 62,947,714 in 1890 to 75,994,575 in 1900 and 91,972,266 in 1910. And, whereas the rural population had constituted 63.9 per cent of the whole in 1890 and 59.5 per cent in 1900, it had dropped to barely 53.7 per cent in 1910.[50] Exports of foodstuffs from the United States had begun to show a steady decline. In 1900 the value of foodstuffs exported was set at $545,473,695; ten years later it was only $369,087,974, and formed but 21.59 per cent of the total domestic exports as compared with 39.8 per cent in 1900, 42.21 per cent in 1890, and 55.77 per cent in 1880. Meanwhile exports of meat and dairy products had declined to $143,000,000 in 1910 as compared with $254,000,000 in 1906 and an average of $222,000,000 during the preceding ten years.[51] Soon all this, and possibly much more besides, would be needed at home. "With our increasing population," said Theodore Roosevelt, "the time is not far distant when the problem of supplying our people with food will become pressing. The possible additions to our arable area are not great, and it will become necessary to obtain much larger crops from the land, as is now done in more densely settled countries." The same idea was expressed by W. C. Brown, president of the New York Central Railroad. "We must increase production per acre by more intelligent methods," he said, "or we must face the relentless certain day when we shall not produce enough to supply our own necessities." Viewing the situation still more pessimistically, James J. Hill of the Great Northern Railroad insisted that "in twenty-five years we shall face a nation-wide famine."[52]

49. *Ibid.*, XXXIV (January 8, 1909), p. 43; XXXVI (September 8, 1911), p. 1219.
50. *Thirteenth Census of the United States, 1910, Abstract*, p. 55.
51. U. S. Dept. of Commerce and Labor, *Reports*, 1910, p. 68. See also *Wallaces' Farmer*, XXXV (February 11, 1910), p. 236.
52. *Report of the National Conservation Committee* (60 Congress, 2 session, Senate Document 676, serial 5397, Washington, 1909), p. 7; *Wallaces' Farmer*, XXXV (February 11, 1910), p. 218; Ruth V. Corbin, "Federal Farm Credits, 1916–1936" (unpublished master's thesis, University of Wisconsin, 1936), p. 2.

In this present day of plenty such acute anxiety about the nation's food supply is difficult to understand, but in the early years of the twentieth century it did not seem unreasonable. The march of industrialization had promoted the growth of population to such an extent that there was in actual fact a relative shortage of food. This condition, to the considerable advantage of the farmer, was reflected in higher food prices. Thanks, at least in part, to the world's increasing supply of gold, there was a generally rising price level, but food prices were rising more rapidly than other prices. This was true not only in the United States, but in Europe as well, and in all other exporting countries. Not until the end of the decade was the balance between population and food supply sufficiently stable to put a check on the rising price of food.

Confident that the nation, if it was to continue to eat, must find some means of stimulating agriculture, publicists began to voice a demand for more effective agricultural education. Theodore Roosevelt, never very far from the head of any procession, urged the cause along. "We should strive in every way," he said, "to aid in the education of the farmer for the farm, and should shape our school system with this end in view."[53] A principal aim of this movement was to promote more scientific methods of farming, but efforts along this line were far from new. Ever since the creation of the Department of Agriculture in 1862, the federal government had participated actively in the scientific study of agriculture and in the dissemination of agricultural information. Colleges of agriculture, subsidized by land grants under the terms of the Morrill Act of 1862, existed in nearly every state not only to carry on direct instruction but also to maintain experiment stations for original investigation and extension divisions for projecting scientific findings beyond the campus to people on the farms. State departments of agriculture and private agencies also did useful educational work. Even so, critics could say that as yet "comparatively little really good farming has been done in the United States. . . . Speaking broadly, we have not even begun to really farm." Only by means of better farming, it was assumed, could the needs of the future for greater quantities of farm produce be met.[54]

53. *Wallaces' Farmer*, XXXII (October 11, 1907), p. 1145.
54. Edwin G. Nourse, *Government in Relation to Agriculture* (Washington, 1940), pp. 872–74; *Wallaces' Farmer*, XXXIII (June 26, 1908), p. 830.

But the believers in agricultural education had more in mind than merely the promotion of better farming methods. They wished also to convince farm boys and girls that farm life offered opportunities comparable with those of city life. Too many farmers still thought of education as a means of providing for their children an easier way of life than farming. As a result, the schools, even the agricultural colleges, some said, were educating farm youth away from the farm. Country schools needed a thorough overhauling. The one-room school with its underpaid, undertrained, and overworked teacher must go. Means must be found to provide for the transportation of children to larger, centrally located schools. Agriculture as a school subject must have an honored place in the curriculum, and teachers must be prepared to present it realistically, in terms applicable to the daily life of farm boys and girls. Prospective farmers must be taught to understand their "own soils, climate, animal and plant diseases, markets, and other local facts."[55] Perhaps an enlarged United States Bureau of Education should restudy all public educational activities and furnish more effective guidance to state and local authorities. All this was supposed not only to make the farmer into a better farmer but also to make him want to stay on the farm. Nevertheless, there was room for the word of warning voiced by an experienced observer:

No matter how much money the government pours out to educate him, he [the farmer] won't be educated except as he educates himself; and his children can not be educated unless he provides better schools than he has now and better teachers than he has now, and takes a greater interest in the education of his own children than most farmers do. No amount of education laid at the farmer's door is going to do him any good unless he takes it with a relish, digests and assimilates it, and puts it actually into practice on the farm.[56]

And yet, taken as a whole, the picture of farm life in the western Middle West during the early years of the twentieth century was by no means discouraging. Agriculture had rarely enjoyed a higher degree of prosperity. Corn growers, wheat growers, and dairymen—farmers of every

55. Senate Document 705, 60 Congress, 2 session, p. 17; *Wallaces' Farmer*, XXXII (August 30, 1907), p. 940; XXXIV (August 20, 1909), p. 1025; XXXV (January 7, 1910), p. 7.
56. *Ibid.*, XXXVIII (January 17, 1913), p. 82. See also Senate Document 705, 60 Congress, 2 session, p. 56.

description—were doing very well. The prices farm products commanded were high, and the unearned increment that came from the increase in value of farm lands added a substantial quota to rural wealth. There were problems to worry about—the increase in tenancy, the shortage of labor, the drift to the city—but they were for the most part problems of prosperity, not of adversity. How could the farmers raise enough to feed the city dwellers? This was an opportunity and a challenge, not a reason for despair. Middle western agriculture was sound, or so, at least, many people believed. Farm mortgages were universally acclaimed as gilt-edged securities, and they commanded low interest rates. Even the federal government was hard at work to keep the farmer prosperous. It provided for agriculture free of charge extensive investigational services that non-agricultural industries had to provide for themselves, and it aided the cause of agricultural education generously.[57] Agricultural discontent was chronic and endemic, but for the moment, at least in the western Middle West, it had less than the normal reason for existence.

57. Nourse, *Government in Relation to Agriculture*, pp. 873–74.

Chapter II

FROM POPULISM TO INSURGENCY

IN SPITE of the prosperity of middle western agriculture during the years that preceded the first World War, the farmer's voice of protest was by no means stilled. During the late nineteenth century western agrarians had built up a philosophy of radicalism sufficient even to endure the acid test of good times. Their experiences with railroads, banks, middlemen, and manufacturers had made them convinced antimonopolists. They were by no means the first to hold antimonopoly views, for the ideas they expressed had often been cogently stated by eastern, or even European, theorists.[1] But the long struggle with frontier poverty, culminating in the Populist revolt, had instilled in many farmers' minds a deep-seated belief that the various combines through which big business operated must somehow be restrained. This attitude was due not to ignorance, but to experience. The farmers knew whereof they spoke. Nor did they have any doubt concerning the role the government must play in providing this restraint. Middle western agrarians were not socialists; on the contrary, they were, or at least they aspired to be, small capitalists. But their property-mindedness did not blind them to the fact that only the power of government could insure them against the unfair advantages of monopoly. They favored government regulation and control, or in extreme cases

1. This chapter follows in the main an article by John D. Hicks, "The Legacy of Populism in the Western Middle West," *Agricultural History*, XXIII (October, 1949), pp. 225–36. For a somewhat different point of view, see Chester McArthur Destler, "Western Radicalism, 1865–1901: Concepts and Origins," *Mississippi Valley Historical Review*, XXXI (December, 1944), pp. 335–68.

government ownership, only as a means of retaining for themselves the right to hold property and to do business on a reasonably profitable basis.[2]

It should be remembered that these rights, throughout the greater part of the western Middle West, were most imperiled by the railroads, and that it was against the railroads more specifically than against any other type of enterprise that the farmers aimed their principal reforms. The railroads had created the region; they had brought the population in; they were in close alliance or even partnership with other industries such as lumber, elevator, milling, and packing corporations; they were the chief exploiters of the farm population, which was obliged to pay them rates both coming and going. When the average middle western farmer living west of Chicago talked about monopolies and trusts, he was thinking primarily of the railroads. Even the towns and cities were peculiarly railroad-conscious. They had no other equally big businesses, and their very lives as trading centers depended upon the fairness, or sometimes the favor, with which railroad rate makers treated them.[3]

Implicit in the Populistic concept of government intervention in economic affairs was the assumption that the government itself should be truly representative of the people, that the long-established control of the "plutocrats" should be broken. The first task that the agrarian leaders set for themselves, therefore, was to capture for the people the machinery of government.[4] It was with this end in view that Farmers' Alliance and Populist candidates sought control of state governments, and that the Populist party nominated J. B. Weaver in 1892 and William Jennings Bryan in 1896 for the Presidency of the United States. Bryan's first defeat rang the death knell of Populism as an effective party organization and served notice on the people generally that the ousting of the "plutocrats" was to be no easy task. But the idea lived on. As Frederick Jackson Turner once phrased it, "Mr. Bryan's Democracy, Mr. Debs' Socialism, and Mr.

2. Benton H. Wilcox, "An Historical Definition of Northwestern Radicalism," *Mississippi Valley Historical Review,* XXVI (December, 1939), pp. 382, 394. This article sets forth the principal findings of the author's more elaborate study, "A Reconsideration of the Character and Economic Basis of Northwestern Radicalism" (unpublished doctoral dissertation, University of Wisconsin, 1933), hereafter cited as Wilcox, "Northwestern Radicalism."

3. Wilcox, "Northwestern Radicalism," p. 50.

4. John D. Hicks, *The Populist Revolt* (Minneapolis, 1931), pp. 405-6.

Roosevelt's Republicanism all had in common the emphasis upon the need of governmental regulation of industrial tendencies in the interest of the common man; the checking of the power of these business Titans who emerged successful out of the competitive individualism of pioneer America."[5] If this end was ever to be achieved, however, the people must somehow take over their government, and the desire to see this ambition achieved survived intact long after the disappearance of the Populist party.

Throughout the western Middle West, and to a considerable extent throughout the country as a whole, this legacy of Populism determined the course of political development during the opening years of the twentieth century. What reforms could be instituted to make sure that the people really governed? The movement for the direct primary, for the initiative and referendum, and for various other instruments of popular government grew naturally out of the soil prepared by the Populists. The campaign to limit the power of the speaker of the national House of Representatives was led by an outraged Nebraskan.[6] The activities of insurgents and progressives generally, culminating in the formation of the Progressive party of 1912, followed an evolutionary pattern easily connected with Populism. This is not to say that the only force that lay back of twentieth-century American radicalism was nineteenth-century middle western agrarianism. The contributions of the labor movement, of imported socialistic concepts, of a host of journalistic muckrakers must not be overlooked. But one extremely important ancestral line—a long and sturdy line—led back to a multitude of Granger-Greenback-Populist progenitors. As convinced antimonopolists, these reformers believed that the state must use its power to regulate and control the "trusts," most of which, in the western Middle West, turned out to be railroads. They believed, too, that if the state was to be charged with this responsibility, its power must be lodged firmly in the hands of the people. Probably they expected greater results from popular rule than was reasonable, but judged by any standards, they did accomplish a great deal. As a result of their efforts "something new had been brought into politics."[7]

5. Frederick Jackson Turner, *The Frontier in American History* (New York, 1921), p. 281.

6. George W. Norris, *Fighting Liberal: The Autobiography of George W. Norris* (New York, 1945), pp. 107–19.   7. Wilcox, "Northwestern Radicalism," p. 107.

Robert M. La Follette of Wisconsin was not a Populist, and the state which furnished the setting for his career was never Populist territory. Yet it would be hard to find another American of the period more thoroughly representative of Middle Western agrarianism or another state more receptive to the idea of governmental regulation of business. A conservative in his earlier years and almost a regular, La Follette had found his hopes for political advancement blocked at every turn by a party machine subservient to the state's industrial leaders. Taking his case to the people, he persuaded a majority of them, farmers for the most part rather than city dwellers, to back him in his war on the bosses. Undoubtedly he was aided in his efforts by the Old World background of many Wisconsin voters, men who were accustomed to a powerful government and now saw no harm in it as long as they could control it. But probably he was aided far more by the strong antimonopoly tradition which among Wisconsin farmers was much older than Populism and dated back to the Grangers. Above all, he furnished to the cause persistent, dynamic, intelligent leadership—something rarely found among the Populists.[8]

La Follette's acknowledgment of his debt to Grangerism is clear and explicit. Progressivism, he maintained, first "expressed itself in the rise to power of the Patrons of Husbandry," whose influence was brief but unique. The Grangers had succeeded in awakening Wisconsin farmers to the possibilities of cooperation; it had made them more sensitive to the abuses operating behind the political and economic scene. "As a boy on the farm . . . I heard and felt this movement of the Grangers swirling about me," wrote La Follette. "I suppose I have never fully lost the effect of that early impression."[9]

In spite of the inspiration he derived from the Grangers, La Follette's decision to lead a movement for agrarian reform did not materialize until he had gone down to defeat as a regular. When he stood for re-election to Congress in 1890, he was serving his third term as a Republican in the House of Representatives. Although showing some evidence of

8. Robert M. La Follette, *La Follette's Autobiography: A Personal Narrative of Political Experience* (Madison, Wis., 1913), p. 18; Theodore Saloutos, "The Wisconsin Society of Equity," *Agricultural History*, XIV (April, 1940), p. 79.
9. La Follette, *Autobiography*, p. 19.

independence, he was sufficiently satisfactory to the party leaders that he had been made a member of the important Ways and Means Committee, and in this capacity he had participated as a believing protectionist in the drafting of the McKinley tariff bill. His defeat for re-election to a fourth term was in part the culmination of a long period of agrarian discontent that swept scores of Republicans out of office throughout the Middle West. In Wisconsin, however, the Democratic landslide was greatly accelerated by the unpopular Bennett law, recently enacted by a Republican legislature.[10] This measure sought to promote a more stringent enforcement of the state's compulsory education laws, and the foreign elements—particularly German, Scandinavian, Irish, and Polish patrons of parochial schools—regarded it as a direct attack on their educational institutions. After his defeat, La Follette decided to confine his immediate political future to the state and began to formulate his plans. Once when asked how he could ever hope to create a truly progressive state out of a nondescript "foreign-born, foreign-bred, slow-moving population," he pointed confidently to the predominance of the agricultural population in Wisconsin and "the absence of great congested centres, which are always the stronghold of machine control through a corrupt combination of big business with municipal graft."[11]

La Follette's full realization of the need for reform probably dated from the day in 1891 when, as he implicitly believed, he was offered what amounted to a bribe by United States Senator Philetus Sawyer, a rich Wisconsin lumberman whose wishes in regard to state politics were generally respected. Out of this ordeal, the facts of which are still in dispute, La Follette emerged with a passionate conviction that he must take the lead in freeing his state from the corrupt influences which were "undermining and destroying every semblance of representative government in Wisconsin."[12] Believing that the mainspring of his reform movement would be found among the farmers, La Follette proceeded at once to ally himself with the outstanding farmer politicians of Wisconsin. Foremost among these was A. R. Hall, "the statesman of the hour immediately preceding the La Follette movement."[13] Hall was a former speaker of the

10. *Ibid.,* pp. 133–34.   11. *Ibid.,* pp. 222–23.   12. *Ibid.,* p. 164.
13. Albert O. Barton, *La Follette's Winning of Wisconsin* (Madison, Wis., 1922), p. 93.

Minnesota house of representatives who had migrated to Wisconsin, and had behind him a long background of agrarian protest. After 1890, when he was elected to the Wisconsin assembly from his new home in Dunn County, he became known for his earnest advocacy of anti-pass legislation, and by 1899 he had won the legislature to his way of thinking.[14]

With equal shrewdness La Follette also made friends with Nils Haugen, a popular Norwegian politician who, although a Republican, had won re-election to Congress in 1890. When Haugen unsuccessfully sought the governorship in 1894, La Follette supported him warmly, and the good feeling thus engendered was not forgotten by the Scandinavian contingent. The Scandinavian farmers, as La Follette well knew, were, next to the Germans, the largest foreign group in the state.[15]

Although La Follette lost in his first try for the Republican gubernatorial nomination in 1896, the returns showed that he had made notable progress in lining up the farmer vote. According to the *Wisconsin Farmer,* a leading farm journal, he was "a man in close sympathy with Wisconsin agriculture." "Such a chief executive," the editorial continued, "is greatly needed in Wisconsin at present. He should be a man, too, with brains and courage, a defender of the 'plain people' and not a tool of corporate interests, nor the choice of corporation lobbyists. . . . We believe that the Hon. R. M. La Follette is such a man."[16] The year following his defeat for governor, La Follette and some of his friends bought out the *Old Dane,* a newspaper for rural readers published at the state capital. Under a new name, the *State,* and with a tow-headed Norwegian, John M. Nelson, as editor, this journal soon became a power in Wisconsin politics.[17] Former Governor William Dempster Hoard, the founder of *Hoard's Dairyman,* was also a La Follette supporter, while two outside newspapers, the *Skandinaven* of Chicago and the *Tidende* of Minneapolis, both of which had many Wisconsin readers, gave him their blessing.[18]

14. La Follette, *Autobiography,* p. 221; *Blue Book of the State of Wisconsin,* 1897, p. 677.

15. Ernest W. Stirn, *An Annotated Bibliography of Robert M. La Follette* (Chicago, 1937), p. 23; K. C. Babcock, *The Scandinavian Element in the United States* (Urbana, Ill., 1914), pp. 166–68.

16. *Wisconsin Farmer* (Madison), July 24, 1896.

17. La Follette, *Autobiography,* pp. 190–91, 207–8.

18. Barton, *La Follette's Winning of Wisconsin,* pp. 55–57.

Meantime, La Follette had discovered in the direct primary an instrument through which the reforms he envisaged could best be accomplished. The direct primary idea, like so many others that the western agrarians found useful, was by no means new, although La Follette professed never to have heard of it until 1896. But whereas earlier efforts to apply this principle had been mainly abortive, La Follette, with the help of the recently adopted Australian ballot, hoped to make popular nominations a living force. The caucus and convention, he maintained, had been "prostituted to the service of corrupt organization." For these outmoded methods he would substitute "a primary election—held under all the sanctions of law which prevail at the general election—where the citizen may cast his vote directly to nominate the candidate of the party with which he affiliates, and have it canvassed and returned just as he cast it."[19] In season and out, during campaigns and between campaigns, he carried this program to the people of the state, and finally in 1900, with the direct primary as a principal issue, he was nominated and elected to the governorship. The completeness of his victory is evident from the fact that he had the unprecedented plurality of 100,000 votes. Beyond a doubt, it was the support of the farmers that had made this signal triumph possible.[20]

But the battle was not yet won. During his first term in office La Follette failed completely to carry a satisfactory primary law through the legislature and was obliged to bring the issue to the people again in his campaign for re-election in 1902. Once more the popular mandate was clear, and this time the legislature yielded, although the bill it finally passed contained a referendum clause designed by opponents of the primary to accomplish its defeat. But the thoroughness with which La Follette's propaganda had done its work was revealed in the election of 1904, when nearly 62 per cent of those who voted on the referendum gave the direct primary their support. At this same election La Follette won a third term.[21]

The first actual use of the primary system in Wisconsin came with the municipal elections of 1905; not until September, 1906, were primary nominations made for state and congressional tickets. Under the Wis-

19. Allen Fraser Lovejoy, *La Follette and the Establishment of the Direct Primary in Wisconsin, 1890–1904* (New Haven, Conn., 1941), p. 36.

20. *Ibid.*, p. 53; A. P. Wilder, "Governor La Follette and What He Stands For," *Outlook*, LXX (March 8, 1902), p. 631.

21. Lovejoy, *Direct Primary in Wisconsin*, pp. 78–79, 83, 90–91.

consin regulations separate primary ballots were provided for each eligible political party. Aspirants for party nominations qualified for a place on the ballot of their choice by obtaining the signatures of a specified number of voters, but each candidate was required to swear that he was a member of the party to whose nomination he aspired and that he would support the candidate who won the nomination for which he contended. Each voter at the polls was presented with a "separate ticket for each party all fastened together," from which he selected and marked one, depositing all others in a blank ballot box. The Wisconsin law, while not the first primary law to be passed, was reputed to be "the first state-wide law with fairly complete provisions for legal supervision." [22]

The direct primary, of course, was designed as a means to other ends, but the La Follette forces did not await its coming before attacking the special interests that had long dominated the state. At the same time that La Follette was promoting the primary elections bill, he was also urging upon the legislature a drastic reform in the method of railroad taxation. Under existing procedure, Wisconsin railroads paid an operating fee, assessed against their gross incomes, in lieu of other taxation. According to the Wisconsin Tax Commission, this meant that they paid only ".53 per cent. of their market value (based on the average value of stocks and bonds)," as compared with the 1.19 per cent paid by real property on its market value. [23] To remedy this condition, La Follette favored the taxation of railroad property on an ad valorem basis, the same as other property, and in 1903 he succeeded, despite the most frantic railroad opposition, in transforming his wishes into law. Nevertheless, every effort was made to be fair to the railroads. When it came to making the new assessment, not only was the market value of railroad stocks and bonds taken into consideration, but these figures were checked with engineers' estimates of the cost of replacement. As the reformers had foreseen, the railroads paid higher taxes. During the first six years the law was in operation the state took in from the railroads about four million dollars more tax money than the roads would have paid under the old system. Furthermore, expert

22. Charles E. Merriam and Louise Overaker, *Primary Elections* (Chicago, 1928), pp. 62, 402; William Francis Raney, *Wisconsin, A Story of Progress* (New York, 1940), pp. 289–90; *Laws of Wisconsin*, 1903, ch. 451, pp. 754–66.

23. La Follette, *Autobiography*, p. 243 .

state accountants searched the books of railroad companies for irregularities and compelled the payment of back taxes upon rebates, generously given but never reported as income.[24]

La Follette was not yet through with the railroads. Railroad rates within the state, he maintained, were unconscionably high. In a "message of 178 printed pages," presented to the legislature on April 28, 1903, he "furnished a final and unanswerable demonstration" that Wisconsin freight rates were from 20 to 69 per cent higher than corresponding rates in the neighboring states of Iowa and Illinois. With the freedom to levy rates they then possessed, La Follette quite plausibly maintained, the railroad companies could easily compensate themselves for higher taxes by passing the bill along to their customers. The proper course, then, was to provide for effective regulation by a railroad commission preferably chosen, so La Follette believed, by the governor. Eventually this reform, despite the usual violent opposition, reached the statute books. In making the appointments it called for, La Follette took pains to select men of broad experience and high standing. The result was that many unfair rates were reduced and many discriminations against communities and individuals discontinued.[25]

The La Follette reforms did not end with the railroads. Other public utilities, such as water, gas, electricity, and telephone corporations, were eventually brought under regulatory control, to their own great distress but to the equally great financial benefit of the public. A stringent Corrupt Practices Act made the use of large sums to influence the results of primary and state elections difficult. An antilobby bill required the official registration of all lobbyists, and even prohibited them from private communications with members of the legislature on matters of legislation. An inheritance tax and a graduated income tax greatly augmented the revenue of the state, enabling it to support educational and charitable institutions far more generously than ever before and also to build a new state capitol, mainly from current revenue.[26] A legislative reference library,

24. *Ibid.*, pp. 291–92; Raney, *Wisconsin*, pp. 290–91.
25. La Follette, *Autobiography*, pp. 280–85, 348–56.
26. *Ibid.*, pp. 297–98, 356–57. It should be noted, however, that during La Follette's administration the State of Wisconsin received a windfall of well over a million dollars from the federal government to cover interest and losses that came from the

designed primarily to furnish legislators with expert advice in the drafting of bills, was established, becoming a veritable hothouse for the growth of progressive measures.[27]

One result of this extensive program of legislation in Wisconsin was a split in the Republican party. Calling themselves "Stalwarts," the regular Republicans—those who saw nothing wrong, either with the old convention system or with the important part played in politics by great corporations—fought persistently against the measures advocated by the Progressives, and tried hard to discredit and defeat Progressive candidates. But the reforms adopted were too popular to be attacked successfully. The heat of controversy lived on, but in time the battle between Stalwarts and Progressives lost much of its meaning. The Stalwarts, generally speaking, came to accept the La Follette measures, and based their opposition on the contention that they alone, as efficient conservatives, were competent to administer them. Even when a Stalwart, Emanuel L. Philipp, was elected to the governorship in 1914, the conditions against which La Follette and his supporters had fought so valiantly were not permitted to return. The Progressives, on their part, were usually content with defending the reforms they had inaugurated, and advanced few new principles.[28]

The activities of La Follette in Wisconsin were speedily paralleled by similar activities on the part of other governors in nearly every other state of the western Middle West. As the direction of the political current became increasingly clear, men of outstanding ability did not hesitate to assume the role of reformer. "Do not fear the title of reformer," Governor Cummins of Iowa told an audience in 1902, "but put true meaning upon the word. The reformer who destroys is the enemy of mankind. The reformer whose cry is 'march on' is the benefactor of his race."[29] What the Populists had failed to develop by way of effective leadership, such

---

disposal of state Civil War bonds below par. This money was added to the general fund and used as if it were income. Raney, *Wisconsin,* p. 294.

27. Edward A. Fitzpatrick, *McCarthy of Wisconsin* (New York, 1944), pp. 43, 62–71.

28. Wilcox, "Northwestern Radicalism," pp. 110–14.

29. Johnson Brigham, "The Governor of Iowa, a Sketch of Albert Baird Cummins," *American Monthly Review of Reviews,* XXXIV (September, 1906), p. 295.

insurgents as La Follette and Cummins, acting through one or the other of the older parties, now provided in generous measure. Indeed, the contagion spread to the entire nation, and an era of reform set in which materially changed the character of state government in the whole United States.

In Iowa, Albert B. Cummins had found his aspirations for a political career blocked by forces similar to those which had fought so tenaciously against La Follette in Wisconsin. A Pennsylvanian by birth, Cummins had read law in Chicago, and in 1878, soon after being admitted to the bar, had opened a law office in Des Moines. He first attracted attention as chief attorney for the Farmers' Protective Association, which sought to break up an offensive barbed-wire combine. This combine, by the simple device of buying up all available patents and then closing competing factories, had succeeded in advancing the price of barbed wire to figures that were obviously exorbitant. For five years, beginning in 1881, through suit after suit, Cummins fought the farmers' battle, until at last he obtained a decision from the Supreme Court of the United States so favorable to his clients that the monopoly was broken.[30]

Cummins' growing interest in railroads led him to give up general practice and specialize in railroad law. His outstanding ability won him clients among the railroad corporations, but they "soon learned that they did not own him."[31] He was never willing to play the role of lobbyist, and as a member of the lower house of the Iowa legislature in 1888 he introduced a "long-and-short-haul" bill that was by no means pleasing to the carriers. During this session, under the leadership of Governor William Larrabee, an outstanding liberal, the legislature enacted a series of reform measures designed to facilitate the regulation of railroads by the state. Cummins participated fully in this program without losing his standing as a regular Republican, but his unwillingness to submit to their control cost him the confidence of the railroads. When he sought election to the United States Senate in 1894, and again in 1896, they branded him as undesirable and defeated him. The excellent showing he made in the

30. *Ibid.*, p. 293; E. W. Harrington, "A Survey of the Political Ideas of Albert Baird Cummins," *Iowa Journal of History and Politics*, XXXIX (October, 1941), p. 340 n.
31. Francis Ellington Leupp, *National Miniatures* (New York, 1918), pp. 105–6.

campaign of 1899, however, was described by the *Iowa State Register* as a "marvel," for he was opposed by "a railroad with millions backing the biggest 'boss' the state ever knew, and a half-dozen allied railroads with the shrewdest men in Iowa political life in their employ, half or more of the congressmen, the entire organization of the great Republican party of Iowa, most of the office holders and aspirants, an army of paid agents, hundreds of influential newspapers whose editors are repaying obligations incurred by accepting postmasterships, and scores of federal office holders whose salaries the nation had paid while they have spent three years in steady, continuous work for their benefactor."[32]

Finally in 1901 Cummins became a candidate for the Republican nomination for governor. His great object, he told one of his opponents, was "to bring the individual voter into more prominence, and to diminish the influence of permanent organization in the ranks of the party." Undoubtedly he had his eye on the United States Senate, but the road to that goal, he decided, lay through the governorship. In a vigorous campaign he denounced the undue influence that the railroads were exerting in the political life of the state and advocated, quite after the pattern set by La Follette in Wisconsin, that a program of primary elections be instituted in order to drive from power the corporations that ruled the state. To make his position doubly clear, he mentioned by name the railway representatives who had long dictated the policies of the Republican party in Iowa, and announced that his candidacy was definitely not by their request. In return for this impertinence they promised to "pound him into the earth," but by this time the people were ready for a change. As a result Cummins entered the nominating convention with a clear majority of the delegates, was nominated on the first ballot, and was later elected at the polls by a plurality of over 83,000 votes.[33]

The first concern of the reform governor, once he had taken office, was to bring the railroads of the state to book. Back in the days of the Farmers' Alliance, with Governor Larrabee in power, a railroad commission had been created, and notable advances had been scored in the establishment

32. Quoted in Fred E. Haynes, *Third Party Movements Since the Civil War, with Special Reference to Iowa* (Iowa City, 1916), pp. 442, 450.

33. *Ibid.*, pp. 451, 454; Harrington, in *Iowa Journal of History and Politics*, XXXIX (October, 1941), p. 347; Jonathan P. Dolliver, "The Forward Movement in the Republican Party," *Outlook*, XCVI (September 24, 1910), p. 167.

of railroad regulation, but some of the gains proved to be only temporary. As public interest in the subject relaxed, the railroads found ways and means to revive their influence. Railroad commissioners, for example, while elected officials, were nominated by railroad-controlled conventions, and they usually turned out to be far more effective in defending the wishes of the railroads than in looking after the interests of the public. Cummins thus found that much of the work done a decade earlier had to be done all over again.[34]

As La Follette was doing in Wisconsin, Cummins began by insisting that the railroads pay a fair share of the state's taxation burden. Railroad assessments, he had maintained during the campaign, should be made "upon the same basis as was applied to farms and city lots."[35] Familiar with every aspect of railroad finance, he was able to dominate the executive council of the state, through which railroad assessments were made. As a result, the total railroad assessment for the year 1902 ran to $4,041,556 more than it had in 1901. To facilitate further the correct evaluation of railroad property, a law of 1902 required that the railroads report to the executive council the net income they derived from business originating in Iowa and terminating in other states, or originating in other states and terminating in Iowa, or neither originating nor terminating in Iowa but carried across a part of the state. All these items were to be included in one lump sum. By the year 1906, railroad assessments in Iowa had been increased by $15,000,000. At the same time, similar increases were made in the taxable valuation of express, telephone, and telegraph companies.[36]

Had the railroad commission of Iowa been an appointive body, as in Wisconsin, rather than an elective body, it is probable that the effectiveness of railroad regulation in Iowa would have been far more marked. The elected commissioners were rarely well qualified for their responsibilities, and they were generally content to take action only on the complaint of citizens rather than on their own initiative. Of some importance was a measure passed by the Iowa legislature, late in the Cummins administration, which authorized the state railroad commission to represent the

34. Haynes, *Third Party Movements*, p. 444; *Wallaces' Farmer*, XXXV (May 27, 1910), p. 824.

35. Haynes, *Third Party Movements*, p. 453.

36. *Appletons' Annual Cyclopaedia*, 1902, pp. 723, 725; Brigham, in *American Monthly Review of Reviews*, XXXIV (September, 1906), p. 292.

people of the state before the Interstate Commerce Commission. When, in 1912, the railroads sought to increase their western rates by 5 per cent, the careful work of Iowa's Commissioner Clifford Thorne had much to do with the retention, at least temporarily, of the old rates.[37]

Although Cummins' record on regulatory legislation was hardly as striking as La Follette's, he managed to make himself thoroughly disliked by the railroads. Possibly his most important action on the railroad question was his veto of the Molsberry bill, through which an increase in the indebtedness of certain Iowa corporations was to have been made easy. The real purpose of this bill, according to former Governor Larrabee, was to turn the state into a "kind of New Jersey" by making the process of "manufacturing corporations" as easy as possible. This veto greatly intensified railroad hostility to the Cummins administration. When Cummins sought a second term, the Standpatters bided their time, but when he chose to violate the Iowa tradition against a third term and run for re-election in 1906, they came out against him in full force and nearly defeated him.[38] Before he left office he had been instrumental in placing on the statute books a two-cent passenger-fare law, a new freight-rate law, a law to limit the hours of railroad employes, and an anti-free pass law.[39]

The strenuous campaign of 1906 may have been the influence that brought Cummins to a really effective support of the direct primary. He had advocated the passage of such a law as early as 1903 and thereafter in his biennial messages of 1904 and 1906. "Wealth, and especially corporate wealth," he had stated in his first message as governor, "has many rights; but it should always be remembered that among them is not the right to vote . . . not the privilege to sit in political conventions or occupy seats in legislative chambers. Corporations, as such, should be rigorously

37. Harrington, in *Iowa Journal of History and Politics*, XXXIX (October, 1941), p. 370; *Wallaces' Farmer*, XXXII (April 19, 1907), p. 533; XXXIV (January 22, 1909), p. 98; XXXV (May 27, 1910), p. 824; XXXVII (February 16, 1912), p. 282.

38. A recent amendment to the constitution of Iowa had designated even-numbered years instead of odd-numbered years for the election of state officers, and had extended the terms of all incumbent officers for one year. Cummins' second term thus lasted three years—from January, 1904, to January, 1907.

39. Harrington, in *Iowa Journal of History and Politics*, XXXIX (October, 1941), pp. 349, 369–70. In his earlier days Cummins himself made free use of railroad passes, and even solicited them.

excluded in every form from participation in political affairs."[40] Cummins' drive for the direct primary in 1907 got results where his earlier efforts had failed. His opponents claimed that his interest in the reform was due in part to his desire to have an expression of the popular will in his impending candidacy for the United States Senate. If so, he must have been greatly disappointed, for when he entered the primaries in 1908 against the aging Senator Allison, he was defeated. Two months later, however, the subject was reopened by the death of Senator Allison, and after a special primary had endorsed Cummins' candidacy, he was at last chosen by the legislature to the office which he had coveted for so long. Meantime, he had recorded his ardent support of an amendment to the national Constitution which would require the election of United States senators by direct vote of the people.[41]

The direct primary was not, of course, the cure-all that many people had hoped it would be. When the time came for voting, the average citizen was likely to be apathetic, while the professional politicians worked without ceasing. Verdicts of the electorate were not always clear-cut. In the Iowa Republican primary of 1908, for example, the Standpat candidates for governor and senator were nominated, while Progressives won the nominations for lieutenant governor and numerous other state and legislative offices. But the results, in general, were good. No longer could it be said, as formerly, that "delegates to political conventions were selected by the railroad attorneys; were dead-headed [by free passes] to the places of meeting, and were then herded and voted by flocks"; or that "delegates were selected by dead-heads, hauled as dead-heads, herded like sheep, and voted as they were told." It is by no means demonstrable that the primary alone broke the back of the old railroad machine; in Iowa, as in Wisconsin, the first important victories of the Progressives were scored before the direct primary was instituted. But undoubtedly the primary system threw the bosses' noses still further "out of joint," and brought "true rule of the people" closer than it had ever been before.[42]

Cummins' interest in national politics clearly had much to do with the emphasis that he placed, while still governor, upon national affairs. One

40. Haynes, *Third Party Movements*, p. 456.   41. *Ibid.*, pp. 464, 467.
42. *Wallaces' Farmer*, XXXIII (June 19, 1908), p. 807; XXXVI (February 3, 1911), p. 162; XXXVII (June 7, 1912), p. 950.

subject that he stressed without ceasing was tariff reform. The Republican state convention of 1900, which contributed the "Iowa Idea" to the age-old tariff controversy, did not abandon the protective principle, but it did advocate "such changes in the tariff from time to time as become advisable through the progress of our industries and their changing relations to the commerce of the world." After endorsing "the policy of reciprocity as the natural complement of protection," the Iowa Republicans went on to advocate "any modification of the tariff schedules that may be required to prevent their affording shelter to monopoly." These last three words—"shelter to monopoly"—were the essence of the Iowa Idea. Neither the language of the platform nor the much-used term, Iowa Idea, were the work of Cummins, but they were both given wide publicity by his frequent public statements. His first and foremost objective, he maintained, was the prevention of monopoly. "I am not an advocate of a general revision of the tariff," he said in his first inaugural address, "but I stand for competition, the competition of the Republic if possible, but of the world if necessary. I regard the consequences of a monopoly, or substantial monopoly, in any important product, as infinitely more disastrous than the consequences of foreign importations."[43]

With reference to the railroads, Cummins again showed his consciousness of the national aspect of the problem. State regulation at best could be only partially effective; by the time a railroad was big enough to need regulation, it was too big for the states to regulate. As early as 1905 Cummins appeared before the Senate Committee on Interstate Commerce to argue for the greater protection of states and localities, as well as individuals, against rate discriminations. Both as governor and as senator he showed genuine interest in restraining railroad monopoly and promoting competition. The disappearance of competition, he believed, only opened the way to socialism.[44]

43. Haynes, *Third Party Movements*, pp. 452–54; see also George E. Roberts, "The Origin and History of the Iowa Idea," *Iowa Journal of History and Politics*, II (January, 1904), pp. 69–82. "It is, of course, not possible to give the farmer protection on very much," wrote the first Henry Wallace, "for tariffs never become operative, no matter what may be on the statute books, when products are shipped abroad in large quantities." *Wallaces' Farmer*, XXXIV (February 12, 1909), p. 221.

44. Harrington, in *Iowa Journal of History and Politics*, XXXIX (October, 1941), pp. 366, 370 n.

The leadership of Cummins in Iowa, like the leadership of La Follette in Wisconsin, revealed a widening rift in the Republican party. The opponents of reform were generally called "Standpatters," and they more or less accepted the designation, while the faction which supported Cummins assumed the more attractive label of "Progressives." In Iowa, no less than in Wisconsin, the reforms that the Progressives adopted were eventually accepted by the opposition, at least as necessary evils. Railroad domination of the Republican party was definitely broken, and the direct primary came to stay. If only Cummins' devotion to the cause of intrastate reform had been greater and his ambition for a career in national politics less, it is possible that he might have accomplished more as governor than he did. He was cautious and deliberate at a time when aggressive tactics would have paid good dividends; some of the most important reforms connected with his name were not put through until after his near defeat for a third term. "A La Follette," wrote Herbert Quick in 1906, "would have at least had the issues made up in less than five years."[45] It is quite possible that the antimonopoly, farmer-minded voters of Iowa were in their thinking well in advance of their leader.

It would have been strange indeed if so pronounced a movement for reform as was manifest in Wisconsin and Iowa had failed to affect Minnesota. Conditions in the three states were much alike, but effective leadership was essential, as the careers of La Follette and Cummins amply demonstrated, if the power of the vested interests was to be broken. Minnesota, ever since Populist times, had suffered from a dearth of able leaders. The men who won high office in the state, while ready enough to give devoted lip service to measures of reform, turned out all too frequently to be mere time-serving politicians, more interested in retaining office than in promoting the principles they preached. Not until the election of 1904, when John A. Johnson, a Democrat, won the governorship in spite of Minnesota's normal Republicanism, was any very genuine progress registered.[46]

Johnson had had no such struggle for political survival as had motivated both La Follette and Cummins, but he had a life story full of emotional appeal. He was the first native Minnesotan, it transpired, ever to hold

45. *Ibid.*, p. 383.
46. Wilcox, "Northwestern Radicalism," pp. 89–91.

office as governor of the state. His parents were humble Swedish immigrants, early settlers in St. Peter, where Johnson was born in 1861. His father, a blacksmith, was unfortunately too fond of drink to provide an adequate living for his family, and therefore young Johnson, because his earnings were needed, was obliged at thirteen years of age to leave school and go to work. Eventually he became interested in journalism, and as the editor of the *St. Peter Herald,* a country newspaper, he gained prominence in his own community. For a single term of four years, 1899 to 1903, he represented his district in the state senate, but his constituency was ordinarily Republican and by a narrow margin he was defeated for reelection.[47]

By this time Johnson had attracted considerable attention throughout the state, partly because of his great personal charm, which won him many friends, and partly because he had shown himself to be an independent thinker who could express himself effectively both in writing and in speaking. When John Lind, the most prominent Democrat in Minnesota, refused to be considered for the Democratic nomination for governor in 1904, the party leaders turned naturally to Johnson, and induced the convention to nominate him by acclamation. His election in the campaign that followed may be interpreted as a kind of popular protest against the petty factional strife and do-nothing tactics of Minnesota Republicans. While Theodore Roosevelt carried the state as Republican candidate for President by a margin of 216,651 to 55,187, the vote for Johnson was 147,992 and that for his Republican opponent only 140,130. Twice thereafter, in 1906 and again in 1908, Johnson won re-election by far more substantial majorities, in spite of every effort on the part of the Republican machine to displace him. His sudden death in 1909 cut short what might have developed into a brilliant career in national as well as state politics.[48]

Johnson was handicapped in his leadership by having to deal, throughout his three administrations, with legislatures opposed to him politically. More important, he could not even count on the support of a sufficient number of reformers to provide the necessary legislative majorities to put

47. William Watts Folwell, *A History of Minnesota* (4 vols., St. Paul, 1921–30), III, 275–76; Frank A. Day and Theodore M. Knappen, *The Life of John Albert Johnson* (St. Paul, 1910), pp. 52–114.

48. *Ibid.,* pp. 119–42; Folwell, *Minnesota,* III, 277–83.

through the reform measures he desired. His victories were therefore incomplete, but his interest in freeing the state from corporation control and in establishing popular government was fully demonstrated. The fact that the people stood by him in one election after another indicates that he felt the public pulse aright. And, with the spirit of reform riding high, Johnson did accomplish a great deal. Undoubtedly one of his greatest assets in obtaining a certain measure of support from Republican legislatures was the fear of the Republicans that the Democrats might get the credit for being more responsive to the current demand for reform than the Republicans.[49]

On the dominant problem of the railroads, Governor Johnson's contributions were somewhat less spectacular than those of La Follette and Cummins. A state railroad and warehouse commission already existed, but its members were reluctant to make full use of the powers they possessed. On one occasion, during the summer of 1906, Johnson was obliged to publicly demand action from the commissioners in order to induce them to so much as grant a request of the three principal railroads of the state to reduce their grain rates by approximately 10 per cent. "One speech of his," according to his biographers, "resulted in a voluntary reduction of ten percent. in certain classes of freight in northern Minnesota." Finally, after the subject of intrastate freight rates had been fully investigated, the legislature, by law, cut the rates on grain, coal, lumber, and livestock an average of 10 per cent. Other railroad measures enacted during Johnson's administration included a reciprocal demurrage law, "subjecting carriers to the same penalties for delay in furnishing cars as carriers impose upon shippers for delay in loading cars," an anti-pass bill, and a two-cent passenger-fare bill.[50]

The Johnson record of reform extended well beyond the railroad sphere. Johnson was deeply interested in the insurance problem, and induced the legislature to pass what "amounted to a code of life, fire, and marine insurance." He also signed measures extending the jurisdiction of the state bureau of labor, industries, and commerce; creating a depart-

49. *Ibid.*, p. 287.

50. Day and Knappen, *Johnson*, p. 159. See also R. W. Oppegard, "Governor Albert Johnson and the Reform Era in Minnesota" (unpublished master's thesis, University of Wisconsin, 1937), pp. 46–48, 52–67.

ment of banking; and permitting cities to own and operate such public utilities as street railways, telephones, water works, gas works, and electric light, heat, and power works. He had little to do, however, with the extension of the direct primary into Minnesota. Like many another state, Minnesota had long made some effort to control the party primaries through which delegates to conventions were chosen, but it took more advanced ground when, as early as 1899, its legislature passed an act for the use of the direct primary in Hennepin County only as a substitute for the customary caucus and convention nominations for city, county, judicial, school, and similarly nonpolitical offices. Two years later this act was extended to the entire state, thus making Minnesota the first state in the Union to require the universal, although strictly limited, use of the direct primary. But it was not until 1912, after the direct primary movement had gathered irresistible momentum, that the Minnesota legislature got around to the enactment of a direct primary law equally applicable to all state offices.[51]

In Missouri the reform governor was Joseph W. Folk. Unlike La Follette, Cummins, and Johnson, who rose to prominence mainly through rural support, Folk first made his name known as the chief law-enforcement officer of a large city, St. Louis. In this capacity, during the years 1901-2, he exposed and prosecuted a group of "boodlers," including the city boss, whose deals with corrupt business interests had cost St. Louis taxpayers princely sums. Twelve of the culprits were convicted and sent to jail. Folk then turned his attention to exposing grafting members of the state legislature and the state administration. The shocking conditions he revealed blasted numerous reputations and made Folk the logical candidate of the Democratic party, to which he belonged, for the governorship in 1904. Nominated less by the support of the cities, where frightened bosses did all they could to defeat him, than by the rural counties, where the spirit of reform was strong, he won the election handily in spite of the fact that the Republicans carried the state in the voting for President and for every other state office except governor.[52]

During his four years in office Folk used the executive power so effec-

51. Folwell, *Minnesota,* III, 287; IV, 366.
52. Lincoln Steffens, *The Shame of the Cities* (New York, 1904), pp. 101-43, and *The Struggle for Self-Government* (New York, 1906), pp. 1-39.

tively that reluctant legislatures were obliged to enact a large number of the reform measures for which the times called—laws for the more effective regulation of the railroads and public utilities, an antilobby law, a direct primary law, and a constitutional amendment making possible the use of the initiative and referendum. The Missouri constitution limited the governor to a single term of four years; thus Folk had no opportunity to run for re-election. His Republican attorney general, Herbert S. Hadley, who had successfully brought suit against three Missouri railroads for combination in restraint of trade and had won an important case against the Standard Oil Company, succeeded Folk as governor and continued in similar vein. Folk, perhaps unwisely, sought election to the United States Senate in 1908, but was defeated in the primary he had helped to establish by the veteran politician, William J. Stone. It is of some significance that Folk carried seventy-four counties to forty for Stone, and that the issue was settled by Stone's decisive victory in the cities. The country population remained loyal to Folk.[53]

What happened in all the other states of the western Middle West differed only in detail. No doubt, as time went on, governors sought consciously to imitate the records of such reformers as La Follette, Cummins, Johnson, and Folk. A reform attitude paid dividends; even the President of the United States, Theodore Roosevelt, had been quick to discover and exploit that fact. In South Dakota Coe I. Crawford turned his back upon his earlier career as railroad lobbyist, sought the Republican nomination for governor upon a platform that was strongly reminiscent of the La Follette demands in Wisconsin, and after a defeat in 1904 at the hands of the machine, won easily in 1906.[54] In Kansas a well-to-do businessman, Walter R. Stubbs, was impressed as a member of the legislature with the inefficiency of state government, and started out to do something about it. Eventually he realized that corporation control was the principal affliction from which Kansas suffered and became an ardent proponent of all the leading progressive reforms. After a decisive defeat by the machine in 1906, Stubbs won nomination and election to the governorship in 1908

53. Frank Warren Crow, "Joseph W. Folk and the Reform Movement in Missouri" (unpublished master's thesis, University of Wisconsin, 1937), pp. 58–84.
54. Doane Robinson, *Encyclopedia of South Dakota* (Pierre, S. Dak., 1925), p. 147.

and served two terms.[55] In North Dakota John Burke, a Democrat, was the reform leader. With the dominant political party, the corporations, and the leading newspapers of the state all against him, he was three times elected governor by excellent majorities—in 1906, 1908, and 1910.[56] In Nebraska, the reform leadership was less personalized, but two progressive Republicans, Norris Brown as attorney general and George L. Sheldon as a member of the state senate, gave some direction to the movement. Campaigning together in 1906 on a reform program, Brown went to the United States Senate and Sheldon was elected governor.[57] In Illinois, Charles S. Deneen, a Republican who held the governorship from 1905 to 1913, was certainly not a spotless reformer, but he at least worked energetically to establish the direct primary. When the supreme court, time after time, invalidated legislation designed to accomplish this end, he stumped the state "county by county, and ward after ward" to secure a law that the court would sustain. Only in 1912, on the fourth attempt, was such a law enacted.[58]

The reforms inaugurated by the legislatures of these states of the Middle West were by no means identical, but clearly marked trends are unmistakable. One type of legislation created, well in advance of most of the other states of the Union, a direct primary system of making nominations for office. This reform was fundamental, and throughout the western Middle West it literally revolutionized state government. Nor was there in this region any such backsliding and evasion as occurred in some of the eastern states. The change had come to stay; candidates were at the mercy of public opinion in a way in which they had never been before. Sometimes, but not always, the direct primary was supplemented by plans for direct legislation—the initiative and referendum. Honesty in politics was frequently sought by means of drastic antilobbying and corrupt practices acts. Direct primaries for candidates for the United States Senate became common, and in some instances a preferential vote, taken at the time of

55. Wilcox, "Northwestern Radicalism," pp. 87–88.

56. *Ibid.*, p. 94.

57. Albert Watkins, *Illustrated History of Nebraska* (3 vols., Lincoln, Nebr., 1905-13), III, 277.

58. Roy O. West, "Charles S. Deneen, 1863–1900," *Journal of the Illinois State Historical Society*, XXXIV (March, 1914), p. 11; Steffens, *Struggle for Self-Government*, pp. 74–78.

the regular election, bound the legislature to accept the candidate designated by the people at the polls. Presidential preference primaries for the
selection of delegates to the national nominating conventions were also
frequently provided, particularly as a result of the candidacy of Theodore
Roosevelt against Taft for the Republican nomination in 1912.[59]

Along with these efforts to promote popular government came much
legislation aimed at the political and economic supremacy of powerful
business interests, particularly the railroads. Expansion of the prerogatives
of railroad commissions, higher corporation taxes, maximum freight rates,
two-cent passenger fares, and anti-pass laws were multiplied in state after
state. It is no exaggeration to say that, for the most part, the peculiar hold
that the railroads had long had upon the political life of the region was
broken. Even the conservative reaction, which began in the western
Middle West as early as 1912, and swept numerous standpatters and
stalwarts back into office, was relatively unimportant, for the only way in
which the conservatives could retain power was to outdo the progressives
in their devotion to the new reforms.[60] The old Populist principle that if
only the people could obtain control of their government, they could
defend themselves adequately against the power of monopoly seemed in
the process of being demonstrated.

The legacy of Populism could easily be traced also into the realm of
national affairs. Such reforms as came to be associated with the name of
Theodore Roosevelt were ardently supported by the agrarian leaders of
the western Middle West, and to some extent, no doubt, were inspired
by them. According to one enthusiast, Roosevelt was the "spokesman of
the people, the expression and exponent of the reform spirit, the mouth-
piece of an awakened conscience."[61] But the westerners wanted to go
much farther than Roosevelt was willing to lead. As La Follette put it,
"He acted upon the maxim that a half loaf is better than no bread. I believe that half a loaf is fatal whenever it is accepted at the sacrifice of the
basic principle sought to be attained."[62] The insurgent movement of the

59. Merriam and Overaker, *Primary Elections*, pp. 62–63, 141–42; Wilcox, "Northwestern Radicalism," p. 107.
60. *Ibid.*, pp. 110–14.
61. *Wallaces' Farmer*, XXXIII (August 14, 1908), p. 976.
62. La Follette, *Autobiography*, p. 388.

Taft administration was even more obviously of agrarian origin. It was, indeed, mainly the work of senators and representatives from the Middle West—men who, according to William Allen White, "caught the Populists in swimming and stole all of their clothing except the frayed underdrawers of free silver."[63] The fight on Cannonism in the national House of Representatives was carried to a successful conclusion through the leadership of such middle western progressives as Norris of Nebraska, Nelson of Wisconsin, Murdock and Madison of Kansas, and Lindbergh of Minnesota. Aid came from some outside supporters, notably Poindexter of Washington and Fowler of New Jersey, but the credit for victory belonged primarily to the middle western agrarians.[64] The assault of the Senate insurgents upon the Payne-Aldrich tariff bill was almost wholly a contribution of the western Middle West. La Follette of Wisconsin, Clapp of Minnesota, Cummins and Dolliver of Iowa, and Bristow of Kansas were the outstanding leaders; only Beveridge of Indiana deserves comparable credit for the work the insurgents did in revealing the monopolistic intent of the Aldrich schedules.[65] In both houses of Congress the insurgents also fought for a graduated income tax, for conservation, for postal savings, for more vigorous railroad regulation, and against a type of reciprocity with Canada designed to benefit the industrial East at the expense of the agricultural Middle West.[66] The overwhelming approval of middle western farm constituencies of the program of the insurgents was repeatedly demonstrated at election time; not only were the radical leaders consistently returned to Congress, but old-guard conservatives were retired with great good will.[67] Eventually most of the reforms for which the insurgents stood found expression in the platform of the Progressive party of 1912, but the candidacy of Theodore Roosevelt blurred the issue and divided their forces. They could not very truly believe in

63. Kenneth W. Hechler, *Insurgency* (New York, 1940), pp. 21–22.

64. *Ibid.*, pp. 33–43.

65. *Ibid.*, pp. 83–91, 145.

66. *Ibid.*, pp. 146–219. Reciprocity with Canada, as proposed by the Taft administration, was, according to one middle westerner, a "jug-handled affair," wholly unsatisfactory to the friends of genuine reciprocity. It "assumes that the farmer owes the manufacturer a living." *Wallaces' Farmer*, XXXVI (March 10, 1911), p. 438.

67. Wilcox, "Northwestern Radicalism," pp. 106–8.

him, nor he in them.[68] But the statement of a close student of the subject that "Wilsonian liberalism and the New Deal were born of Insurgency" carries no appreciable discount.[69]

68. George E. Mowry, *Theodore Roosevelt and the Progressive Movement* (Madison, Wis., 1946), pp. 269–73.
69. Hechler, *Insurgency*, p. 221.

Chapter III

EARLY PHASES
OF THE COOPERATIVE MOVEMENT

WHILE the early years of the twentieth century saw much evidence of the farmers' influence in politics, it must not be supposed that more direct methods of farmer action were overlooked. Chief among these was the development of farmer cooperatives, especially those designed for the marketing of dairy products, grain, and livestock. Long experience had convinced many farmers that too large a percentage of the prices ultimately paid by the consumer went to the middlemen and other handlers of farm produce rather than to the farmers themselves. According to one reliable estimate, the farmers' share of the consumer's dollar varied from 35 to 50 per cent, while the other 50 to 65 per cent went to transportation companies, wholesalers, and retailers. Small wonder that a subscriber wrote in to the editor of *Wallaces' Farmer:* "Had you not better take up the subject of how to market our produce, rather than to tell us all the time how to produce more?"[1]

Beginning in about 1900, cooperatives in the United States took a new lease on life, achieving their greatest successes, except for the strong movements in California and New York, among the dairy, grain, and livestock producers of Minnesota, Wisconsin, Illinois, and Iowa. In all these states the cooperatives showed remarkable increases in the numbers of

1. *Wallaces' Farmer,* XXXII (April 19, 1907), p. 534; XXXV (December 2, 1910), p. 1734; XXXVII (November 29, 1912), p. 1682.

cooperative organizations, the length of their membership lists, and the volume of their sales and purchases. The reasons for this development are complex and varied, including, among others, (1) a favorable trend in court decisions, (2) state and federal legislation for the legalization of cooperatives, (3) the demonstrated success of cooperative undertakings abroad as well as at home, (4) the desire of farmers to emulate the efficient methods of distribution achieved by business and industry, (5) the endorsement of cooperatives by prominent men in all walks of life, (6) the multitudinous activities of a variety of state and federal agencies, and (7) the hue and cry of untold millions—farmers and nonfarmers alike—for money-saving reforms in distribution.

Statistics provided by the federal government, although far from complete, indicate that during the late nineteenth century the greatest progress in the use of cooperatives had been made in the twelve north central states, nine of which comprise the western Middle West. By the year 1900 there were, mostly in these states, about 2,000 farmers' business organizations. Of these, nearly 1,600 were cooperative creameries or cheese factories, while about 100 were grain elevators and a similar number were devoted to the marketing of fruits. Of the 200 other farmer enterprises, some were engaged in the marketing of livestock or other farm produce and some were cooperative stores. The total business that these cooperatives transacted was estimated at only a little less than $200,000,000. As the years elapsed the volume of cooperative activities increased greatly, but the relative importance of the western Middle West as a cooperative center remained unchanged.[2]

The growth of cooperatives in the western Middle West owed a great

2. R. H. Elsworth, "A Quarter Century of Cooperative Development," *Cooperative Marketing Journal*, I (December, 1927), pp. 30–31; Federal Farm Board, *Statistics of Farmers' Selling and Buying Associations, United States, 1863–1931*, Bulletin 9 (Washington, 1932), pp. 7–9. For greater details on the status of cooperatives in different states and periods, see other studies of Ralph Henry Elsworth: *Development and Present Status of Farmers' Cooperative Business Organizations*, U. S. Dept. Agri., Agricultural Bulletin 1302 (Washington, 1925); *Agricultural Cooperative Associations, Marketing and Purchasing, 1925*, U. S. Dept. Agri., Technical Bulletin 40 (Washington, 1928); *Cooperative Marketing and Purchasing, 1920–1929*, U. S. Dept. Agri., Circular 121 (Washington, 1930); *Statistics of Farmers' Cooperative Business Organizations, 1920–1935*, Farm Credit Administration, Bulletin 6 (Washington, 1936).

deal to the long procession of farm organizations that flourished in this region—the Grangers, the Farmers' Alliance, the American Society of Equity, the Farmers' Union, the American Farm Bureau Federation, and numerous independent groups. The pioneer work was performed by the nineteenth-century orders, but their twentieth-century successors built upon the old foundations and exploited the same old farmer grievances. Mounting discontent over commission charges, dockage, grading, poor service, short weights, lack of competition among dealers, low prices, and the generally high marketing costs made the task of persuading the farmers that their salvation lay in the establishment of their own marketing machinery easy. From such a system they might hope to obtain a greater share of the consumer's dollar, a need particularly felt by all farmers who lived long distances from their markets and by small operators who were obliged to purchase and sell uneconomically in less than carload lots.[3] Immigrants such as the Norwegians, Swiss, and Danes of Wisconsin, Minnesota, and the Dakotas—many of whom were familiar with co-operatives in the Old World—often, but not necessarily always, responded favorably to propaganda for group action.[4]

While it is true that cooperatives had made their greatest progress in the western Middle West, the forces that had stimulated their growth were by no means solely confined to this region. Perhaps too great importance is attached, however, to the oft-cited example of the English consumers

3. The literature of this subject is extensive. See particularly E. G. Nourse, "Fifty Years of Farmers' Elevators in Iowa," *Iowa State Agricultural Experiment Station, Bulletin 211* (Ames, Iowa, 1923), pp. 236–51; E. G. Nourse and C. W. Hammans, "Cooperative Livestock Shipping in Iowa in 1920," *ibid., Bulletin 200* (1920) pp. 403–4; "Cooperation in Kansas," *Nineteenth Biennial Report of the Kansas State Board of Agriculture* (Topeka, 1915), pp. 154–81, 199–224; Henry H. Bakken and Marvin A. Schaars, *The Economics of Cooperative Marketing* (New York, 1937), pp. 2, 47–62 (especially pp. 49–51); P. R. Fossum, *Agrarian Movements in North Dakota* (Baltimore, 1925), pp. 51–83; Theodore Macklin, "Cooperation Applied to Marketing by Kansas Farmers," *Kansas State Agricultural Experiment Station, Bulletin 224* (Manhattan, Kans., 1920), pp. 7–8, 47–61; Herman Steen, *Coöperative Marketing* (New York, 1923), pp. 4–7; DeWitt C. Wing, "Trends in National Farm Organizations," U. S. Dept. Agri. Yearbook, *Farmers in a Changing World* (Washington, 1940), p. 964; Joseph G. Knapp and J. H. Lister, *Cooperative Purchasing of Farm Supplies,* Farm Credit Administration, Cooperative Division, Bulletin 1 (Washington, 1935).

4. Edward A. Ross, *The Old World in the New* (New York, 1914), p. 91.

who in 1844 had banded themselves together to form the Rochdale Society. Cooperative ventures, although generally unsuccessful, had been tried on this side of the Atlantic before the Rochdale group was organized, and at least one, a group of Wisconsin cheese producers, is credited with having achieved success as early as 1841 in the cooperative manufacture of cheese.[5] The Rochdale pioneers, important as they were in the history of cooperatives, were organized as urban consumers to economize on their purchases and not as sellers of farm produce. The success of their system rested upon two fundamental principles: (1) the acceptance of the prevailing market price in the sale of goods to patrons, and (2) the distribution of profits to members in proportion to the amounts of their purchases. Their program was woven of the same fabric as those of the Owenites, the Chartists, and the advocates of the Reform Bill of 1832. They were part and parcel of an urban movement bent upon rectifying or bettering the unfavorable situation of the unemployed or poorly paid urban workers rather than a rural movement seeking lower marketing costs and higher returns from farming.

The position of the Wisconsin cheese makers was more nearly typical of the producers of the western Middle West. They cooperated not "because of poverty and want" but rather to increase their profits.[6] Indeed, the farmers as producers and sellers and the consumers as purchasers and utilizers tended inevitably to gravitate toward opposite sides of the bargaining counter. The consumers, whether Rochdale pioneers or cooperators of a less distinguished line, were interested in purchasing their commodities at the lowest possible price, while the farmers who had banded

5. Steen, *Coöperative Marketing,* pp. 4, 156–57. Chapter 13 is entitled "America's First Coöperators." See also *Cooperation in Foreign Countries* (68 Congress, 2 session, Senate Document 171, serial 8397, Washington, 1925), p. xi. It was here reported that "The cooperative is of such magnitude and importance . . . that it challenges attention. More than 285,000 organizations in all parts of the world are connected with it." The number of people represented by cooperatives was placed at more than 30,000,000.

6. George J. Holyoake, *Self-Help by the People, The History of the Rochdale Pioneers* (London, 1900), pp. 2–3; Sydney R. Elliot, *The English Cooperatives* (New Haven, Conn., 1937), pp. 6–40. See also Henry W. Brown, *The Rochdale Pioneers; The Story of the Toad Lane Store, 1844, and the Origin of the Cooperative Union,* 1869 (1931); Robert A. Campbell, "Coöperation in Wisconsin," *American Review of Reviews,* XLVII (April, 1913), p. 468.

together in cooperative marketing associations sought the highest possible returns.[7]

Whatever their foreign antecedents, the marketing cooperatives of the western Middle West had to face the practical, everyday problems that the American farmer confronted. He had troubles with railroads, with middlemen, and with financial institutions: cooperative associations had to deal with the same difficulties. Before they could succeed, there had to be much "experimentation in selecting, borrowing, adapting, contriving and fitting together devices, procedures and arrangements" into the kind of organization that would do the work required of it. So many elements of the modern business corporation had to be adopted that the cooperative which eventually appeared has been described as in outward form "a business corporation and in the end a mutual benefit society."[8] According to one authority, the marketing cooperatives had no "special techniques"— "they simply imitated the practices of the private business organizations with the important modification that the gains or advantages should accrue to those who participated in the enterprise." The fact that cooperative leaders often made reference to the efficient methods of distribution employed by American industrialists seems to indicate their very strong interest in trying to profit from these examples. Three principal characteristics emerged as the identification marks of a genuine cooperative: first, it must be democratically controlled; second, it must set reasonable limits on its capital; and third, it must distribute its earnings on the patronage basis.[9] But these characteristics alone would hardly have been

7. John Hanna, The Law of Cooperative Marketing Associations (New York, 1931), p. 4; Bakken and Schaars, The Economics of Cooperative Marketing, pp 169–70. See also Steen, Coöperative Marketing, pp. 3–4. According to Steen, "The spectacular success of the Rochdale society led to the application of the Rochdale plan to agricultural coöperation. This was the case in Great Britain and Ireland, and through northern Europe, notably in the Scandinavian countries. It failed for farmers almost as completely as it had succeeded for the factory workers of Great Britain, and for a quarter of a century agricultural coöperation stood still in Europe. Then American farmers revived and perfected the old Swiss system of coöperative marketing and its success led to its general adoption in European agriculture."

8. Walton H. Hamilton, "Judicial Tolerance of Farmers' Cooperatives," Yale Law Journal, XXXVIII (May, 1929), pp. 938–39; W. S. Harwood, "Cooperation in the West," Atlantic Monthly, LXXXV (April, 1900), pp. 539–40; George Harold Powell Coöperation in Agriculture (New York, 1913), pp. 10–12.

9. Bakken and Schaars, The Economics of Cooperative Marketing, pp. 146–47

adequate to insure the success of a typical American cooperative. The American pattern generally combined good business practices with the Rochdale principles.

Nevertheless, every effort was made to find out what the English and European cooperatives were doing, and to adapt their methods to the needs of the movement in the United States. Commissions and individuals were sent abroad; data were collected; reports were submitted; and recommendations were made. But there is little tangible evidence that much of lasting importance resulted from these investigations. Inevitably they led to the holding of conferences, the passing of resolutions, and the depositing of materials in archives. But it was one thing to collect data and confer and resolve and quite another to influence the course of the cooperative movement.[10]

Probably more potent than the study of foreign procedures were the recommendations of President Theodore Roosevelt's Commission on Rural Life. The commission, besides emphasizing the need for cooperatives, called attention to the obstacles which impeded their growth, and designated the regions of undiversified one-crop farming as the place of their greatest need. The commission also urged upon the states the necessity of passing enabling legislation and upon Congress the desirability of promoting cooperatives in every way it could, particularly with respect to cooperative rural credits.

Naturally, the advocates of farmer cooperatives made good use of the

---

At the bottom of page 146 the authors cite "practices commonly used by American cooperatives [which] are not distinguishable from those of private business corporations." Melvin T. Copeland, interestingly enough, treats the topic of cooperative marketing under the broad general heading of "Marketing" in *Recent Economic Changes in the United States, Report of the Committee on Recent Economic Changes of the President's Conference on Unemployment* (2 vols., New York, 1929), I, 374–89.

10. *Agricultural Cooperation and Rural Credit in Europe* (63 Congress, 1 session, Senate Document 214, serial 6519, Washington, 1913); Senate Document 171, 68 Congress, 2 session; *Agricultural Cooperation and Rural Credit in Europe, Report of the American Commission* (63 Congress, 2 session, Senate Document 261, serial 6570, 2 vols., Washington, 1914); *Adaptation of the European Cooperative Credit System to Meet the Needs of the American Farmer—Report of the International Institute of Agriculture on the Conference Held at Nashville, Tenn., April 1912* (62 Congress, 2 session, Senate Document 855, serial 6178, Washington, 1912).

commission's findings. Farm groups and agricultural leaders saw to it that those phases of the report which favored cooperatives received wide circulation. There was nothing revolutionary or startling in these findings and recommendations; for the most part they only repeated charges and demands that farmers had been making all along. But the endorsement given to cooperatives by President Roosevelt and his commission did make a difference. The members of the commission—L. H. Bailey, Henry C. Wallace, Kenyon Butterfield, Walter H. Page, Gifford Pinchot, and Charles Barrett—were all well known in farm circles, and their warm approval of cooperatives helped place the hood of respectability upon them.[11]

The support given the movement by Sir Horace Plunkett, the prominent Irish cooperative leader, also lent prestige. Plunkett had come to the United States to regain his health, and had made the acquaintance of leaders all over the country. Even after his return to Ireland he was a frequent visitor to the United States. He exchanged views on cooperatives with President Roosevelt and with Gifford Pinchot. He also became acquainted with Charles McCarthy, the state legislative librarian in Wisconsin—a student of cooperation and a prominent figure in progressive Republican politics. Of his association with McCarthy Plunkett wrote, "I have had the privilege of assisting him to draft the Co-operative Law (which partly answers to our Industrial and Provident Societies and Friendly Societies Acts) for his State." Plunkett addressed the Wisconsin legislature in 1911 and again in 1913, and held conferences with "the Governor, with State officers, with the president of the University, and with the dean and faculty of the College of Agriculture." He subscribed heartily to the Roosevelt formula of "better farming, better business, better living," but urged that first emphasis be placed on the "better business" side of farming, because it was there that the farmers were most wanting.[12]

11. *Report of the Country Life Commission* (60 Congress, 2 session, Senate Document 705, serial 5408, Washington, 1909), pp. 128–37, 150. One of the recommendations of the commission was that the cooperatives might "establish prices and perhaps to control the production." This sounds like the work of Barrett.

12. E. F. Baldwin, "Two Leaders in Rural Progress," *Outlook*, XCVI (December 10, 1910), pp. 829–30; Horace C. Plunkett, "McCarthy of Wisconsin," *Nineteenth Century*, LXXVII (June, 1915), p. 1346; Campbell, in *American Review of Reviews*, XLVII (April, 1913), p. 468; Horace C. Plunkett, *The Rural Life Problem of the United States* (New York, 1910), pp. 86–87.

Unfortunately, the legal status of cooperatives in the United States was long the subject of heated controversy. Before the enactment of legislation specifically legalizing cooperatives, the practice of the farmers had been to organize as best they could under the corporation laws of their respective states. These laws, however, were designed for a different purpose and did not fit the cooperative need; moreover, they left the cooperatives open to the danger of prosecution under the antitrust laws, which forbade conspiracy in restraint of trade.[13] Farm organizations such as the Grange had long emphasized the need for constructive legislation on this subject, but their efforts to achieve a special status for horticultural and agricultural organizations did not at first achieve satisfactory results. In the case of *Loewe* v. *Lawler* (1908), when the United States Supreme Court was asked to invoke the Sherman Anti-Trust Act against labor organizations seeking higher wages and agricultural organizations striving for higher prices, the Court held unequivocally against the labor unions and the cooperatives. The act, it maintained,

. . . had made no distinctions between classes. It provided that "every" contract, combination, or conspiracy in restraint of trade was illegal. The records of Congress show that several efforts were made to exempt organizations of farmers and laborers from the operations of the Act, and that all these efforts failed, so that the Act remained as we have it before us.[14]

This point of view caused the advocates of cooperatives much distress. Between 1890 to 1910 many attempts were made to prosecute the directors and officers of selling cooperatives. Indictments against such individuals were brought in five states under state antitrust laws, and in Louisiana an indictment was brought under the Sherman Act. While none of the defendants were convicted, as charged, of fixing prices, the farmers were left in grave doubt regarding the legality of their efforts to create and operate effective marketing cooperatives.[15]

13. H. W. Ballentine, "Cooperative Marketing Associations," *Minnesota Law Review*, VIII (December, 1923), p. 2. See also Hamilton, in *Yale Law Journal*, XXXVIII (May, 1929), pp. 938–39; Steen, *Coöperative Marketing*, pp. 3–4; Hanna, *Law of Cooperative Marketing Associations*, p. 4.

14. 208 U. S., 274, p. 301. See also Franklin J. Jones, "The Status of Farmers' Cooperative Associations Under Federal Law," *Journal of Political Economy*, XXIX (July, 1921), pp. 595–96; Knapp and Lister, *Cooperative Purchasing of Farm Supplies*, p. 24.

15. John D. Miller, "The Philosophical and Legal Background of the Cooperative

Fortunately, this unfavorable legal situation was not to endure unchanged. In spite of the stand taken by the Supreme Court, the weight of judicial opinion held that under the common law farmers had a perfect right to organize for collective marketing and purchasing. There was also a tendency to admit that the antitrust statutes "were enacted to correct abuses which had developed in the collective activities of other groups" and not among the farmers. While the *Loewe* v. *Lawler* decision was not the last of its kind, the view that eventually won out was that not all combinations restricting competition were necessarily illegal, especially if their object was to foster trade and increase business and not to "exercise improper control or unduly and unreasonably restrict competition." The test of illegality came to be whether they abused their power. By the time the Clayton Anti-Trust Act of 1914 was passed, farmer and labor organizations were strong enough to obtain the exemption of nonstock, nonprofit labor, agricultural, and horticultural organizations from the operation of the national antitrust laws. But the cooperative leaders were not satisfied with this victory; they also needed, and in some instances had already obtained, the specific and positive legalization of farmer cooperative associations organized for mutual benefit.[16]

Two states of the western Middle West—Wisconsin and Nebraska—took the lead in 1911 with the first really modern legislation on the subject of cooperatives. Needless to say, these laws were hardly the first statutes to deal with the problem. Minnesota, for instance, had passed a simple law on cooperatives as early as 1870, and had improved on it steadily thereafter. Likewise California and Alabama had "nonstock laws," and Kentucky had enacted a "pooling" statute. But the legislation of Wisconsin and Nebraska was more nearly fundamental than any that

---

Movement in the United States," The American Institute of Cooperation, *American Cooperation, 1935* (Washington, 1935), p. 16.

16. *Ibid.*, p. 15; Ballentine, in *Minnesota Law Review*, VIII (December, 1923) pp. 9–10; Jones, in *Journal of Political Economy*, XXIX (July, 1921), pp. 595–96 M. O. Tobriner, "Cooperative Marketing and the Restraint of Trade," *Columbia Law Review*, XXVII (November, 1927), p. 827. Frequently cited were two Iowa decisions which held that certain Iowa organizations were restraints in trade. *Reeve* v. *Decorah Farmers' Cooperative Society*, 160 Iowa 194 (1913), 140 Northwestern Reporter 844 (1913); *Ludoewese* v. *Farmers' Mutual Cooperative Co.*, 164, Iowa 19 (1914), 145 Northwestern Reporter 475 (1914).

had preceded it. Of the two laws, the Wisconsin statute was newer and broader in concept in some ways and had wider influence, serving eventually as the basis for similar legislation to be adopted in a dozen other states. It provided that any number of persons greater than five might organize for cooperative purposes; that the shares of each stockholder were not ordinarily to exceed one thousand dollars; that each stockholder was entitled to only one vote, which might be cast by mail; that dividends were paid in proportion to patronage; and that only associations living up to these provisions might designate themselves as cooperatives. The Nebraska law was mainly short and permissive, but it laid down the requirement that earnings be distributed "in part or wholly on the basis of, or in proportion to, the property bought from or sold to members, or of labor performed, or other service rendered to the corporation."[17]

The farmers, to qualify for the special treatment they obtained under these laws, had to satisfy the legislators of two things: first, that their associations and business agencies were not monopolies; and second, that the farmer's calling was unique compared with other businesses and hence was in need of special legislation to survive. There was an abundance of evidence on both points. It could easily be demonstrated that all efforts to perfect monopolies in the major agricultural industries were sure to meet with insurmountable difficulties. Open membership in the associations militated against monopoly. The inevitable tendency of millions of small producers to increase their output with the rise of prices also worked against monopoly. Lack of capital and problems of geography made monopoly practically impossible. As for the second point, farming was "different." Other industries enjoyed the benefit of concentrated production under single management in a factory system, whereas the farmer was isolated in his work. As a bargainer, the farmer was inexperienced; he was "ignorant of his fellow farmer's operations, of the quality, the grade, the character of the general crop, of his foreign and

17. Bakken and Schaars, *The Economics of Cooperative Marketing,* p. 272; Edwin G. Nourse, *The Legal Status of Agricultural Cooperation* (New York, 1928), pp. 46–47; Nourse, "The Growth of Cooperative Law," *Cooperative Marketing Journal,* I (December, 1926), p. 10; Hanna, *Law of Cooperative Marketing Associations,* pp. 31–33; B. H. Hibbard, "Agricultural Cooperation," *University of Wisconsin Agricultural Experiment Station, Bulletin 238* (Madison, 1914) [see pages 3–31 for a copy of the Wisconsin law of 1911].

domestic market, of general trading and credit conditions." His dependence on nature gave him little voice in any attempt to regulate the output. On these grounds supporters of agricultural interests based their plea for special treatment fitted to the farmer's "peculiar needs."[18]

Wisconsin and Minnesota also enacted legislation requiring the collection of information about cooperatives. In Minnesota, by a law of 1913, the department of agriculture of the University of Minnesota was required "to collect statistics and information in reference to cooperative associations among farmers and the management and methods of conducting such associations."[19] The Wisconsin legislation antedated this and was more ambitious. The Wisconsin State Board of Public Affairs, especially created for the purpose in 1911, was authorized, in conjunction with the Legislative Reference Library, to make a careful investigation of cooperation. "This investigation was made with three objectives in mind—first, to ascertain the extent and present status of cooperation in Wisconsin; second, to learn the causes for the success of existing cooperative organizations and causes for the failures of those that had not been able to withstand the struggle; and third, to see what lessons could be derived from abroad and how they could be applied here."[20] Possibly this action indicated an awareness of the fact that the responsibility for improving the business side of farming should not be left to sentimentalists, promoters, and more or less erratic farmers, but instead should be taken over by people who wanted to investigate the field in its entirety and to proceed along scientific lines.

The federal government gave slight attention to the farmers' marketing problems until the farmers themselves had taken the initiative in setting up their associations and had exerted considerable political pressure in their respective states. The Department of Agriculture, for the most part, had contented itself with impressing upon the farmers the necessity for bettering the quality of their produce and increasing it in quantity. Never-

18. Tobriner, in *Columbia Law Review*, XXVII (November, 1927), pp. 828–31; Tobriner, "The Constitutionality of Cooperative Marketing Statutes," *California Law Review*, XVII (November, 1928), pp. 25–26.

19. L. D. H. Weld, "Statistics of Cooperation among Farmers in Minnesota," *University of Minnesota Agricultural Experiment Station, Bulletin 146* (St. Paul, 1914), p. 3.

20. Campbell, in *American Review of Reviews*, XLVII (April, 1913), p. 470.

theless, the department had taken a few preliminary steps in the direction of improving the farmers' marketing conditions. It had gathered some information on the subject, had developed techniques for dealing with it, and had trained the necessary personnel for the study of the problem.[21] It had even made a study, in 1911–12, of a few cooperative cotton associations, and had furnished them with some suggestions for the improvement of the methods they employed in the handling and marketing of cotton. But with the creation of the Office of Markets and Rural Organization in 1913 there was a change of pace. Thereafter the collection of statistical information on cooperatives became a major undertaking.[22]

During these early years the state colleges of agriculture contributed even less than the United States Department of Agriculture to the growth of cooperative marketing, and, even harder to understand, they showed an astonishing indifference to the whole subject of agricultural economics. The guiding policy of the colleges of agriculture in the earlier days had been to make two blades of grass grow where only one had grown before and to apply "a knowledge of the laws of the 'natural' sciences to the practical operations of the farm." Of the state universities in the western Middle West, the University of Wisconsin was among the first, if not the first, to offer a course in the "Economics of Agriculture." This course, conducted by Professor William A. Scott "especially for agricultural students," was listed in the university catalogue as early as 1892–93.[23] Three or four years later, the Office of Experiment Stations of the United States Department of Agriculture sponsored a committee on instruction in agriculture which reported that rural economics should be recognized as a division of the science of agriculture. The treatment of the subject by the

21. J. T. Horner, "The United States Governmental Activities in the Field of Agricultural Economics Prior to 1913," *Journal of Farm Economics*, X (October, 1928), pp. 451, 458–59.

22. Chastina Gardner, *Cooperation in Agriculture*, Farm Credit Administration, Cooperative Division, Bulletin 4 (Washington, 1936), p. 5. See also Thomas Nixon Carver, "The Organization of Rural Interests," U. S. Dept. Agri., *Yearbook*, 1913, pp. 239–58.

23. *Catalogue of the University of Wisconsin*, 1892–93, p. 60. Two courses were listed for most of the years down to 1902–3: "Agricultural Economics," designed for students in the short course in the college of agriculture, and "General Course in Agricultural Economics." *Ibid.*, 1902–3, p. 94.

committee admittedly was crude and tentative, yet it did stimulate some interest.[24] In general, however, progress was slow. In 1903, one prominent rural educator observed that "beyond elementary work in economics, in civics, and occasionally in sociology, little opportunity is given students to study the farm question from its social standpoint. With few exceptions, these institutions offer no courses whatever in rural social problems, and even in these exceptional cases the work offered is hardly commensurate with the importance of the subject."[25]

When the colleges of agriculture did begin to act, it was in Wisconsin and Minnesota, where the cooperative movement had reached significant proportions, that the first serious beginnings were made. T. L. Haecker, of the University of Minnesota Agricultural Experiment Station, launched his campaign for the establishment of cooperatives as early as 1891, but it was not until 1908-9 that the University of Minnesota listed a course on the "Economics of Agriculture," dealing with such subjects as markets, prices, transportation, farm ownership, size, organization, and the labor system. In 1902-3 the University of Wisconsin offered a course in agricultural economics under the instructorship of Henry C. Taylor, thereby blazing a path for which its college of agriculture was to become justly famous. Taylor's book, *An Introduction to the Study of Agricultural Economics,* the first to bear in its title the term "agricultural economics," appeared in 1905. But in spite of its title, Taylor's text had no section dealing with marketing, rural finance, agricultural labor, wages, standards of living, cost of transportation, taxation, or related problems.[26] By 1911 Professor C. J. Galpin of the University of Wisconsin began his studies in

24. Alfred C. True, *A History of Agricultural Education in the United States, 1785-1925,* U. S. Dept. Agri., Misc. Publication 36 (Washington, 1929), p. 253.

25. Kenyon L. Butterfield, "American Agricultural Education," *Popular Science Monthly,* LXIII (July, 1903), pp. 257-58.

26. *Report upon the Survey of the University of Wisconsin: Findings of the State Board of Public Affairs and its Report to the Legislature* (Madison, [1915]), pp. 949-50; Andrew Boss, "Minnesota Agricultural Experiment Station, 1885-1935," *University of Minnesota Agricultural Experiment Station, Bulletin 319* (St. Paul, 1935), pp. 34-35; *The College of Science, Literature, and the Arts, 1908-1909,* University of Minnesota Bulletin (Minneapolis, May 26, 1908), p. 100; Edwin G. Nourse, "Agricultural Economics," in *Encyclopaedia of the Social Sciences* (15 vols., New York, 1930-35), I, 534-35.

the problems of rural Wisconsin, and two years later Professor B. H. Hibbard of the same institution gave the first extensive course in cooperation and marketing. That same year Professor George F. Warren of Cornell published a notable book entitled *Farm Management*. These three schools—Minnesota, Wisconsin, and Cornell—were well in the lead on these subjects. Most agricultural colleges, as late as 1914, had not even started to investigate them, or else had made only "a gingerly beginning, in abstract, general ways."[27]

Since cooperatives developed chiefly in regions specializing in the production of a particular commodity, it was hardly surprising that the first successful cooperatives to be found in any number were among the dairy producers. By the year 1900 no less than 549 dairy associations had been organized in the United States, most of them during the last decade of the century.[28] By 1915 the number of dairy cooperatives exceeded those of any other commodity. Minnesota then had more dairy associations than any other state; Wisconsin ranked second, and Iowa third; but by 1925 Minnesota and Wisconsin had changed places. In 1915 the Minnesota cooperatives had the most members, with those in Wisconsin and Iowa next in line; but by 1925, New York had jumped into the lead, with Minnesota, Wisconsin, and Pennsylvania following in the order mentioned. In 1915 Wisconsin ranked first in the amount of the cooperative business transacted, trailed by Minnesota, Iowa, and Michigan. But by 1925, Minnesota had moved into first place, New York into second, Wisconsin into third, and California into fourth. Most of the shifts in position that occurred during this decade can be accounted for by the relative growth of the cooperative marketing of fluid milk.[29]

The first organizations of dairy producers were effected in order to manufacture cheese and butter on a cooperative basis. As early as 1810, the dairy producers of Connecticut had made unsuccessful efforts to organize; and it appears on fairly good authority that it was a group of farmers in Rock Lake, Jefferson County, Wisconsin, who in 1841 first banded together to form a "cheese ring" to manufacture their cheese on

27. *Survey of the University of Wisconsin,* pp. 945, 947–49.
28. F.F.B., *Statistics of Farmers' Selling and Buying Associations,* p. 4.
29. Elsworth, *Agricultural Cooperative Associations,* pp. 36–37.

a cooperative basis. These "cheese rings," because they saved labor and commanded better prices for their product, soon began to appear in great numbers in Massachusetts, New York, and Wisconsin.[30]

Wisconsin made rapid strides as a cooperative cheese-manufacturing state. Favorable climatic and topographical conditions, a growing foreign demand, and the coming of Swiss immigrants helped the cheese industry off to a good beginning. The influx of the Swiss, beginning about 1845, into Green County and the adjoining parts of Iowa and Lafayette counties contributed greatly to the growth of cooperative cheese making, but the knowledge, skills, and habits of these people were not enough to reproduce the Swiss cheese industry. Superior Swiss cheese required a milk of higher quality than that used to make ordinary cheddar, limburger, or brick. When economic forces compelled an adjustment to geographic conditions, the cheese factories had to locate "on the highlands to the west and along the Lake Michigan shore counties to the northeast."[31] Furthermore, the "old dairy farm" system of production soon began to give way to the cheese factory, which was better equipped, reduced wastage and manufacturing costs, and produced a more nearly uniform product for market. Freed from the work of cheese making at home, the dairy farmer was now able to keep more cows and to give them better attention than ever before. It was estimated that in 1915 there were 718 cooperative and 1,211 private cheese factories in Wisconsin.[32]

Once the dairy producers had succeeded in manufacturing their cheese

30. *Cooperative Marketing* (70 Congress, 1 session, Senate Document 95, serial 8859, Washington, 1928), p. 7; for early data on cooperative cheese production in the United States, see Steen, *Coöperative Marketing*, pp. 156–57.

31. S. M. Babcock and H. L. Russell, "The Cheese Industry: Its Development and Possibilities in Wisconsin," *University of Wisconsin Agricultural Experiment Station, Bulletin 60* (Madison, 1897), pp. 5–6; H. C. Taylor and C. E. Lee, "Progress of the Dairy Industry in Wisconsin," *ibid., Bulletin 210* (1911), pp. 24–26. See also H. L. Russell, "Dairy Industry in Wisconsin," *ibid., Bulletin 88* (1901); O. E. Baker, "Agricultural Regions of North America," *Economic Geography,* II (October, 1926), p. 464; Glenn T. Trewartha, "The Green County, Wisconsin, Foreign Cheese Industry," *ibid.,* (April, 1926), pp. 292–308.

32. E. H. Farrington and G. H. Benkendorf, "Organization and Construction of Creameries and Cheese Factories," *University of Wisconsin Agricultural Experiment Station, Bulletin 244* (Madison, 1915), p. 3; B. H. Hibbard and Asher Hobson, "Markets and Prices of Wisconsin Cheese," *ibid., Bulletin 251* (1915), pp. 24–28 (see map on page 22).

cooperatively, they logically turned their attention to marketing it in the same way. In the beginning, the factories sold individually to country buyers who purchased on their own account or as representatives of dealers in central markets. As the industry developed, cheese boards sprang up at various points where buyers and sellers met, generally once a week, to transact business. The boards, in line with what happened in the purchase and sale of other commodities, established base prices for the purchase of cheese. Eventually the cheese board at Plymouth, Wisconsin, made up of important cheese dealers and producers, came to dominate the market and became the chief factor in determining the price of cheese in the United States.[33]

Equally important in Wisconsin was the cooperative marketing of butter. A survey conducted in 1914 by the Wisconsin State Dairy and Food Commission revealed that 380 creameries were cooperatively owned. Two years later these cooperatives represented 45 per cent of all the creameries in the state and paid the farmers better than three cents a pound more for their butterfat than the prices offered by the private creameries; they also paid their buttermakers $10 a month more than the wages current in the private creameries. The cooperatives were able to do this because they could command a higher price for their butter; also, they were in a better position than the private owners to control the quality of their cream.[34]

The development of the cooperative creamery movement in Minnesota was equally remarkable. In this state dairying began first to supplement, then to supplant the raising of wheat. As has already been noted, the name of Theophilus Levi Haecker loomed large in the history of Minnesota's dairy industry. Born of German immigrant stock in Ohio on May 4, 1846, Haecker moved with his parents to Dane County, Wisconsin, seven years later. Here he eventually acquired a reputation as a dairy farmer and made the acquaintance of William R. Taylor, the Granger governor of Wisconsin. Haecker became a leader in local Grange affairs;

33. Senate Document 95, 70 Congress, 1 session, p. 10; Steen, *Coöperative Marketing,* pp. 158–63.

34. B. H. Hibbard and Asher Hobson, "The Marketing of Wisconsin Butter," *University of Wisconsin Agricultural Experiment Station, Bulletin 270* (Madison, 1916), pp. 3–11, 66–69.

he joined in cooperative marketing and purchasing activities, helped organize a cooperative creamery and subsequently a cooperative fire insurance venture. As a clerk in the governor's office for seventeen years, Haecker developed a keen appreciation of public needs and became closely identified with a movement to promote a "more practical education" for the students of the University of Wisconsin's college of agriculture. In 1891, Haecker himself enrolled in the university's department of dairy husbandry, reputedly the first of its kind in the world. His superiors immediately recognized his practical knowledge of buttermaking; first he was made an assistant and later he was placed in full charge of "the home dairy work." That same year he went to the University of Minnesota as an instructor in buttermaking.

On moving to Minnesota, Haecker recommended that the farmers there make butter the main product of the state. In the manufacture of cheese, they would be unable to compete with Wisconsin, with its more advantageous freight rates. On Haecker's urging, the Minnesota dairy school placed its principal emphasis on high-quality butter and the control of conditions surrounding buttermaking. A short course was established to train the older men who were already engaged in the industry, while the full-school-year courses prepared the younger men. It is estimated that some 2,500 creamery operators, trained in the dairy division of the University of Minnesota, were influenced directly or indirectly by Haecker's training.[35]

Haecker knew the history of cooperative experiments in Wisconsin well, from Granger times on down, and was particularly impressed by the program of a Danish community at Clarks Grove in Freeborn County, Minnesota. With this as a model, he took steps to promote the cause of cooperative creameries throughout Minnesota. To answer requests for information, he prepared a bulletin, "Organizing Co-operative Creameries," which was published by the University of Minnesota Agricultural Experiment Station. This marked the beginning of a development which was not to stop until the Minnesota producers became nationally famous. When Haecker began to advocate cooperatives, there were probably not more than four cooperative creameries in Minnesota. Ten years later the

35. E. E. Edwards, "T. L. Haecker, The Father of Dairying in Minnesota," *Minnesota History,* XIX (June, 1938), p. 149–57.

number was almost double that of any other state and nearly one-third of the total in the country. In 1914, 42 per cent of the Minnesota farmers were patrons of the cooperative creameries, which comprised 72 per cent of all creameries in the state. Because of this situation, the butter industry in Minnesota was controlled by the farmers to a greater degree than in any other state. These cooperatives, after about thirty years of operation, formed the foundation for the Land O'Lakes Creameries, Incorporated, "probably the greatest butter marketing organization in the world."[36]

The cooperative movement among the dairy producers of Iowa was far behind those of both Wisconsin and Minnesota. Lacking the high quality of leadership which characterized the movements in these states, it endured a long period of trial and error. Nevertheless the Iowa dairy producers had certain common grievances which tended to bind them together. They were often kept waiting a full month before they learned the quality of the milk they sold and almost an equally long time before they knew what prices they were to be paid. If they objected to the price, there was little they could do about it; if there was any inaccuracy, waste, or dishonesty in handling their produce, all they could do was to complain, or go elsewhere and be treated worse. The cause for "nine-tenths" of the Iowa dairy farmer's dissatisfaction, according to one observer, was suspicion over the testing of his milk. Efforts to regulate the method of testing proved unsuccessful, and the discontented farmer, however groundless his suspicion, was on the alert for some means to redress the grievance he felt. Nor was this the only complaint. Sometimes the farmer suffered from insufficient competition among dealers, sometimes from excessive competition. Sometimes there was a lack of satisfactory outlets. The "one-price system" of paying for butterfat also caused great indignation. Often farmers producing high-grade cream received no premium whatsoever, a policy which naturally checked any incentive to improve the quality.[37]

Once the advantages of the cooperative creamery became apparent, whether in Iowa or elsewhere, promoters of various types began to invade

36. Boss, in *Minnesota Bulletin 319,* pp. 34–35; Weld, in *Minnesota Bulletin 146,* p. 6–7.

37. Iowa Department of Agriculture, *Iowa Yearbook of Agriculture,* 1902, pp. 171–73; Frank Robotka and Gordon C. Laughlin, *Cooperative Organization of Iowa Farmers' Creameries,* Farm Credit Administration, Cooperative Division, Bulletin 4 (Washington, 1932), p. 1.

the field and plague the producers. Perhaps the situation in North Dakota during the first decade of the twentieth century was typical. Promoters, representing manufacturers of creamery machinery and equipment, encouraged farmers to build creameries in communities where not enough milk could be produced to support them. Real estate agents, eager to draw in settlers from the eastern dairy states, aided the promoters, regardless of the disaster that would inevitably follow. The promoters were merely interested in making cash sales, while the real estate agents cared little whether the creamery failed or succeeded, if only they could make land sales. Nearly 40 per cent of local creameries in North Dakota were built at the instigation of outside promoters. It should have occasioned no surprise that creameries established under such conditions failed. Out of 133 creameries established in the state between 1888 and 1923, not less than 107 failed, mostly because of the excessive competition between creameries for an inadequate supply of cream. Other trouble came from poor management, dishonest officials, and poor workmanship.[38]

Perhaps more representative of middle western agrarian discontent than the dairy farmers' cooperatives, and eventually more numerous, were the local grain-marketing associations. The organizations of these locals took on exceptional earnestness about 1900, and over the next twenty years nearly 4,000 of them were set up to receive and ship grain.[39]

The roots of the cooperative grain-marketing movement are to be found in the unfavorable marketing conditions which accompanied the expansion of wheat growing following the Civil War. During the seventies, the Grange had been instrumental in organizing a number of grain elevators, many of them cooperative, but largely because of mismanagement nearly all of them failed after a few years of operation. This left the country grain business in the hands of independent dealers who competed with one another fiercely, with disastrous results for many operators. Among the problems that perplexed them were overbidding for grain, dishonesty among weight masters and commission men on the primary market, and leaky cars which lost much of the grain en route to the market.

38. Alva H. Benton, "Marketing Dairy Products," *North Dakota Agricultural College Experiment Station, Bulletin 182* (Agricultural College, N. Dak., 1924), pp. 11–15.

39. F.F.B., *Statistics of Farmers' Selling and Buying Associations,* pp. 4, 43, 71.

To remedy this situation, the tendency was for a large number of dealers to join together in associations. By employing inspectors and grain masters to look after the interests of the group, they succeeded in checking many of the abuses. Once success was realized, the grain dealers did not always use their power to the advantage of the farmer. They made track buyers, for example, whom they had always looked upon with disfavor, the special object of their displeasure. Track buyers could quote higher prices for grain than other purchasers because they had little capital invested, paid no taxes, and stayed in business only while conditions were favorable. In one fashion or another the dealers' associations managed to squeeze them out.

Also of great importance in the grain trade were the activities of the commercial line companies, backed as they were by the abundant capital of exporters and commission firms and favored also by the railroads along which their elevators were located. Often the managers and large investors in these lines were stockholders or directors of the railroads that served them; hence the way was wide-open to special treatment, including cheaper rates. Line companies, when they chose, could make conditions intolerable for the independents. Sometimes they offered to buy an independent elevator outright, and if the owner refused, company officials might even threaten to build a new elevator and "run him out." Compelled to choose between financial ruin and compliance with the line companies' requests, hundreds of independents in the upper Mississippi Valley were obliged to choose the latter alternative.

Farmers soon detected a high degree of uniformity in the prices that the line companies offered them; only when local competitive conditions forced them to it did the line companies pay high prices. A. J. Hoskins, the price agent for a group of 39 elevator companies controlling from 900 to 1,000 elevators in Minnesota and the Dakotas, testified before the Interstate Commerce Commission in 1906 that he received from a committee representing the companies daily price quotations which he, in turn, communicated to the local elevators.[40]

The system of country grading and inspection of grain was another constant source of discontent. Local agents examined the farmers' grain

40. Oscar N. Refsell, "The Farmers' Elevator Movement," *Journal of Political Economy*, XXII (November, 1914), pp. 874–85.

for weed seeds, dirt, shrunken kernels, and other foreign materials, and then decided the allowance for dockage to be deducted. The method in common use was to pass a sample of the grain through a sieve and by a series of siftings to separate out the refuse. Weighing the grain to determine its grade was the next step; for this a "hand tester" or "test kettle" was used. Once the grade and weight had been determined, a price per bushel was offered.

According to the Federal Trade Commission, the highly competitive character of the country grain trade had forced many agents, seeking grain for their respective companies, to overgrade the grain offered them and then to resort to heavy allowance for dockage and underweighing in order to offset the overgrading. This became the practice especially when the farmer threatened to take his grain to a neighboring elevator. A sympathetic agent, often influenced by the deep-seated rural prejudices against the line company which he represented, or possibly by having himself been a farmer, or, as was very common, by having relatives who were farmers, was naturally tempted to overgrade the grain. And, since grading was largely a matter of individual judgment, the agent could hardly be taken to task for what he had done.[41]

But whatever favors were shown the farmer in the grading of his grain were generally more than offset by the system of cleaning grain that was customary. Farmers who cleaned their grain before hauling it to market had less of a problem than those who depended on the elevator for this service. Sometimes the dockage was returned to the farmer, who paid a charge for the cleaning of his grain; in other cases, the elevators performed the service gratis. Neither of these methods caused any difficulty, because in both instances the dockage was returned to the farmer. But there was trouble when the elevator kept the dockage and gave the farmer nothing for it. In defense of this practice it could be argued that the elevator was entitled to the dockage in compensation for the services it provided.[42]

The exact beginnings of the cooperative grain-elevator movement are unknown. It is well established that the Grange, the Farmers' Alliance,

41. *Report of the Federal Trade Commission on the Grain Trade* (7 vols., Washington, 1920–1926), I, 99–103; *The Application of Dockage in the Marketing of Wheat*, U. S. Dept. Agri., Farmers' Bulletin 919 (Washington, 1917), pp. 3–4.

42. F.T.C., *The Grain Trade*, I, 8–9, 204–6.

and the Farmers' Mutual Benefit Association were in the vanguard of the movement. Farmer elevators were in existence in Iowa during the sixties, in Kansas and Minnesota during the seventies, and in the Dakotas by the nineties.[43] Specific information on their existence in Wisconsin and Illinois is slight, yet the presumption is very strong that they were in existence in both states during these early years. In Iowa, where the grain-marketing activities were undoubtedly representative of those in other states, the earliest of the farmer elevators began its short career in Blairstown about 1867 or 1868, one or two years before the state Grange was established.

The majority of the early cooperative elevators were incorporated as regular stock companies, and the others as voluntary associations; there were few evidences of the payment of patronage dividends or the employment of other standard cooperative practices. There was a tendency, however, to limit the amount of stock issued and to restrict control to the organizers.[44]

The decline in the cooperative elevator movement, which set in following the first flush of Granger enthusiasm, revealed some serious defects in methods of organization and operation. The most common fault was insufficient funds, but some of the cooperatives failed because they had been set up in areas where a shift was in progress from wheat to livestock raising. An inadequate grasp of the complexities of the grain business, Granger politics, and rivalry for office added to the difficulties of the cooperatives, made competition with private grain dealers difficult, and contributed to the mortality rate.[45]

The spread of the Farmers' Alliance during the 1880's witnessed an earnest effort to re-establish the farmers in the grain business. This second period of cooperative activity found the private grain interests stronger and more firmly entrenched than ever before; it was, indeed, a period in which combinations both in industry and in transportation were the order of the day. Faced by stronger opposition, the cooperatives sought to adopt a stronger form of organization and to devise means to secure the

43. Nourse, in *Iowa Bulletin 211*, p. 236; *Nineteenth Biennial Report of the Kansas State Board of Agriculture* (1915), pp. 24, 155–56; Fossum, *Agrarian Movements in North Dakota*, p. 161. See also Senate Document 95, 70 Congress, 1 session, p. 54.

44. Nourse, in *Iowa Bulletin 211*, pp. 236–39.

45. *Ibid.*, pp. 239–40.

permanent support of their members. The most novel of the innovations was the "maintenance" or "penalty clause," which provided that any member who sold to a private dealer was required to compensate the cooperative elevator by paying into its treasury a specified sum, usually from one-half to one cent per bushel on all grain sold. At least four Iowa farmers' elevators are known to have adopted such clauses during the eighties and nineties: one in Marcus in 1887 and three others in Rockwell, Rockford, and Rock Valley in 1889, 1891, and 1892, respectively. The object of the penalty clause was to bind the farmers to their own elevators, and to some extent it seems to have succeeded. In spite of the continued opposition of the line companies and the hard times of the 1890's, the cooperative movement endured. In Iowa alone it has been estimated that between 1897 and 1903 from two to seven elevators were organized each year, despite the persistent and well-organized opposition.[46]

The success of the cooperatives in dealing with their opponents is well illustrated by events that transpired in Iowa following the organization in 1900 of the Iowa Grain Dealers' Association. This association provided for a union of forces between the independent dealers and the line companies, who together considered themselves entitled to the entire grain business. Through the association these two groups entered into agreements over prices and the sharing of all available business. But the farmer cooperatives were quick to retaliate. Meeting in Rockwell in November, 1904, the representatives of seventeen farmer elevators launched a counter-association known as the Iowa Farmers' Grain Dealers Association. The object of this new agency was to assist farmers who wanted to handle their own grain business in the formulation of suitable by-laws and in the adoption of sound methods of operation. The success of its propaganda is attested by the fact that the number of farmer elevator companies in Iowa grew from 30 in 1904 to 511 in 1921. Aid of various kinds was offered by the state association: legal advice, commercial information, an auditing service, information regarding competent managers, advice on the selection of elevator sites and the erection of buildings. As the farmer elevators grew in numbers, their bargaining strength won them better treatment from the railroads and from terminal purchasers. They also had a large part in the passage of the Iowa cooperative law of 1915. By 1913

46. *Ibid.*, pp. 241–46.

similar associations had been formed in six out of the nine states of the western Middle West. In the Nebraska state association, organized in 1903, grain and livestock producers joined forces to form the Farmers' Cooperative Grain and Livestock Association.[47]

Thus, despite all opposition, the farmer elevator movement continued to grow. From Illinois and Iowa it had spread into the Dakotas, Kansas, Minnesota, Nebraska, Wisconsin, and Indiana. Besides being engaged in the marketing of grain, some, but by no means all, of the farmer elevators handled coal, lumber, farm implements, bricks, drainage tile, flour and feed, binder twine, oils, kerosene, and gasoline. Some elevators also traded in livestock. In general, the establishment of a farmers' elevator at any given point meant a higher local price for grain, and as knowledge of this fact grew, the cooperative movement grew with it.[48]

With better control of their grain market assured, the farmers turned their attention increasingly to the great central terminal markets at Chicago, Minneapolis, Omaha, Kansas City, St. Louis, Duluth, and Milwaukee—the nerve centers of the grain business. Here were located the headquarters for all the large buyers and sellers, for the principal banks that financed the grain trade, and for the transportation companies that handled the grain. Here, too, were large accumulations of grain, stored in terminal elevators. Whatever the grievances of the farmers against the country system of grading, weighing, and cleaning, they were insignificant in comparison with those that might, and often did, arise on the terminal scene. With the growth in volume of cooperative business, the attitude of the terminal commission firms toward the farmer elevators tended to become more and more friendly. Commission firms that had formerly refused to do business with the cooperatives began to solicit their business eagerly, while those who had always been friendly to the farmers' movement flourished as never before. But the usual mixing, grading, and inspection practices at the terminals still gave rise to much farmer dissatisfaction, and the railroads were by no means free from the charge of discrimination.[49]

47. *Ibid.*, pp. 246–51. See also Refsell, in *Journal of Political Economy*, XII (December, 1914), pp. 977–78.
48. *Ibid.*, pp. 986–87.
49. *Ibid.*, pp. 978–79; Senate Document 95, 70 Congress, 1 session, p. 61.

The difficulties faced by farmer associations which tried to break into the terminal market before 1920 appear in the history of two such companies—the Equity Cooperative Exchange of St. Paul and the Farmers' Cooperative Commission Company of Hutchinson, Kansas. The Equity Cooperative Exchange of St. Paul, in spite of its name, was incorporated in North Dakota in 1911 and began its business operations in Minneapolis. There it became involved in endless difficulties with representatives and sympathizers of the Minneapolis Chamber of Commerce. It moved to St. Paul in 1914, where it set up a grain exchange and began to acquire a line of seventy or eighty local elevators scattered throughout the Dakotas, Minnesota, and Montana. Never a stable organization, the exchange experienced an endless procession of internal bickerings and litigation until it was forced into the hands of receivers in 1923. The second terminal marketing cooperative, the Farmers' Cooperative Commission Company, began operations in Hutchinson, Kansas, in 1915; in 1928, it claimed to own, operate, and control no less than fifty-four local companies and sixty country elevators. The company owned memberships on the boards of trade in Kansas City, Missouri, and in Wichita, Hutchinson, and Dodge City, Kansas. Both the Equity Cooperative Exchange and the Farmers' Cooperative Commission Company encountered their greatest opposition when they sought to obtain membership on boards of trade, for private dealers particularly resented the cooperative practice of disbursing patronage dividends. But eventually the farmers obtained state and federal legislation which prohibited boards of trade from discriminating in this way against cooperatives.[50]

Impressive as their accomplishments were, the grain-marketing cooperatives were probably not as effective as the associations formed for the marketing of livestock. In this activity the farmers of Minnesota, Wisconsin, Iowa, Nebraska, and Kansas were the pioneers. In these states the multiplication of local associations was most rapid during the years 1910 to 1920; in the latter year their volume of shipments attained record breaking proportions. In Iowa alone on January 1, 1921, there were 61

50. *Ibid.*, pp. 61–63; Theodore Saloutos, "The Rise of the Equity Cooperative Exchange," *Mississippi Valley Historical Review*, XXXII (June, 1945), pp. 31–6; Steen, *Coöperative Marketing*, pp. 213–14; Senate Document 95, 70 Congress, session, pp. 62–63.

livestock-shipping associations, plus 37 farmer elevators which bought and shipped livestock, thereby bringing the total up to 647. In Wisconsin the number in 1920 was placed at approximately 500 locals. The figures in Minnesota for 1919 show 655 locals in operation. More than one-fourth of the livestock shipped from the state of Iowa was handled by farmers' marketing organizations, while 75 per cent of the livestock sent into the South St. Paul market, and about 15 per cent of all that reached the Chicago market, was shipped by cooperative associations.[51]

In livestock marketing, as in grain marketing, both the Grange and the Farmers' Alliance had made important beginnings. Associations were organized in Iowa, Missouri, Nebraska, and Illinois during the years 1872 and 1873. Most of them were managed by agents of the Grange and operated mainly as selling agencies. As interest in the Grange declined, interest in the associations disappeared also, and few of these early cooperatives survived. Farmers' Alliance livestock cooperatives were active in Kansas, Nebraska, Iowa, and Missouri during the middle 1880's, but with the collapse of the Alliance and the growing farmer interest in politics, the livestock-shipping movement slackened.[52]

In the period from 1903 to 1920, the American Society of Equity and the Farmers' Union took the lead in furthering the livestock cooperative movement. Equity, directly or indirectly, was responsible for the establishment of associations at Postville, Iowa, in 1904, at Durand, Wisconsin, in 1906, and at Litchfield, Minnesota, in 1908. The Farmers' Union began its operations several years later in Nebraska, southern and western Iowa, Kansas, and Missouri. Iowa was ideally located for the movement to flourish. The state was surrounded by seven principal livestock markets and had within its borders, or close to them, eleven minor packing centers. Thus it could distribute its surplus hogs, cattle, and sheep to the various markets with the maximum of efficiency and a minimum of cost

51. E. G. Nourse and J. G. Knapp, The Co-Operative Marketing of Livestock Washington, 1931), pp. 17–19; Nourse and Hammans, in Iowa Bulletin 200, pp. 04, 407; B. H. Hibbard, L. G. Foster, and D. G. Davis, "Wisconsin Livestock hipping Associations," University of Wisconsin Agricultural Experiment Station, ulletin 314 (Madison, 1920), pp. 3–5; E. C. Johnson and J. B. McNulty, "Livestock Shipping Associations in Minnesota," University of Minnesota Agricultural xperiment Station, Bulletin 302 (St. Paul, 1934), p. 3.
52. Steen, Coöperative Marketing, pp. 92–93.

and wastage. The earlier success scored in organizing cooperative cream-eries and grain elevators, plus the fact that local shipping associations were comparatively simple to organize and finance, helped promote their rapid progress.[53]

The chief incentive for the establishment of cooperative livestock ship-ping was the system of country buying then in use. The farmers com-plained bitterly of the wide margins of profit exacted by buyers, stock-yards, and commission firms, the discriminatory nature of their prices, and their generally unfair trade practices. There was a strong conviction that marketing costs somehow had to be lowered. Before the local shipping associations assumed permanent form, it had been a common practice among farmers to join together in making up a carload shipment. Out of the success of these spasmodic and occasional efforts grew the decision to establish permanent marketing associations. In this instance, the associa-tion could be formed without either capital or plant. All that was needed was to assemble the livestock and ship it to market; the association itself assumed no risks by purchasing stock outright. Expenses were low, and an elaborate system of accounting was unnecessary.[54]

The advantages which the shipping associations offered the farmers best explain the rapidity of their growth. Livestock producers who shipped cooperatively got the market price, minus a minimum cost for marketing, and thus made larger profits. This was the case also in the handling of miscellaneous stock like canners or veals, when uniform shipments of stock could not be made. By shipping cooperatively, producers also became better acquainted with the market and the grades; they found it less dif-ficult to get cars for shipments even in periods of shortages; they could ship their livestock whenever it was ready, without having to wait for a buyer to see it; they saved themselves much time and labor by the em-ployment of a single manager; they obtained close to the market price for crippled livestock, which previously they had sold for half price; they learned that excessive losses from death, shrinkages, and injuries en route

53. Nourse and Knapp, *The Co-Operative Marketing of Livestock*, pp. 13–14; Nourse and Hammans, in *Iowa Bulletin 200*, pp. 403, 407–8; E. Dana Durand, "Cooperative Livestock Shipping Associations in Minnesota," *University of Minne-sota Agricultural Experiment Station, Bulletin 15* (St. Paul, 1916), pp. 6–8.

54. Nourse and Knapp, *The Co-Operative Marketing of Livestock*, pp. 45–48; Durand, in *Minnesota Bulletin 15*, pp. 6–8.

o market could be avoided by not overfeeding their stock; they observed
that better animals brought better prices, hence saw new value in scientific
breeding; they got better treatment in the central market because of the
larger volume handled; and finally, they enhanced the prosperity and
the reputations of their local communities.[55]

The formation of local shipping associations in large numbers led
naturally to the establishment of terminal livestock-marketing associations. And essentially the same reasons that induced the farmers to create
local livestock cooperatives drew them into the terminal field. Here high
commission rates, unfair discrimination in the services rendered, and the
variety of prices paid spurred the livestock producers to compete with
private firms.

The earliest farmer attempts to set up cooperative terminal agencies
were by no means successful. One of the first such efforts was the Amer-
can Live Stock Commission Company, organized in 1889. The share-
holders in this company were the Farmers' Alliances of Kansas, Nebraska,
nd Missouri and the Kansas state Grange. Beginning operations in May,
1889, it soon had commission firms operating on the Chicago, Kansas
City, St. Louis, and Omaha markets. With a paid-up capital of $25,000,
y November 30, 1889, the company had some $40,494 in profits to divide
among its stockholders. For the year which ended December 1, 1890, it
collected more than $101,000 in commissions at the four markets and sold
more than $2,500,000 worth of livestock. At first the Chicago manager
was able to obtain a membership on the Chicago livestock exchange but
his was soon lost, and without it the company was unable to operate in
that center. The closing of the Chicago market was disastrous to the
whole organization, and soon the other markets were also abandoned.[56]

Typical of other early failures was the Co-operative Live Stock Commission Company, organized under the laws of Colorado with a capital
stock of $100,000. This company began business at Chicago and Kansas
City on September 1, 1907, but speedily aroused the anger of the private
firms by displaying a profit. The discriminations which followed led to

55. Hibbard, Foster, and Davis, in *Wisconsin Bulletin 314*, pp. 7–9.
56. C. G. Randall, *Cooperative Marketing of Livestock in the United States by
Terminal Associations*, U. S. Dept. Agri., Technical Bulletin 57 (Washington, 1928),
p. 6–7.

a decline in its business and substantial financial losses. Eventually the company had to cease operations.[57]

Later efforts were more successful. Indeed, by the time the first World War broke out, the task of forming a cooperative of any kind had become far less difficult than in the formative years. This was due in considerable part to the provisions of the Clayton Anti-Trust Act and to the laws of the various states for the legal protection of cooperatives. The years 1915 to 1921 saw the formation of more farmers' cooperative associations than any like period either before or since. By 1921, according to one estimate the number of such associations in the United States had reached a total of 12,000. Terminal livestock companies caught on in the new era along with the rest.

The Equity Cooperative Exchange established a terminal agency on the South St. Paul market in 1916, and two years later it began operation in Chicago. In 1917 the Nebraska Farmers' Union organized commission firms on the Omaha and the South St. Joseph markets; the following years Farmers' Union terminal agencies appeared in Sioux City, Iowa and Kansas City, Missouri. Over the period 1917 to 1925, some twenty-five terminal agencies were established on a successful basis throughout the nation.[58]

One significant development that reflected the mounting interest in cooperatives was the government-sponsored credit system suited to the needs of agriculture.[59] Despite sharp differences over the actual credit needs of the farmers, there was a strong feeling that the existing credit institutions discriminated against them; that the farmers were in reality without organized credit; that they were obliged to pay interest rates that were far too high.[60] The Country Life Commission recognized this sit-

57. *Ibid.*, p. 8.   58. *Ibid.*, pp. 46–53, 101.

59. William I. Myers, *Cooperative Farm Mortgage Credit, 1916–1936*, Farm Credit Administration, Cooperative Division, Circular A8 (Washington, 1936), pp. 5–6.

60. Jesse E. Pope, "Agricultural Credit in the United States," *Quarterly Journal of Economics*, XXVIII (August, 1914), pp. 727–28. In critical vein, Pope wrote ". . . there is an utter lack of adequate information as to the actual credit needs of the farmer and of the extent to which existing agencies are supplying them. . . Credit agencies in great variety have come into being in the United States to meet the demands of an undeveloped, unstandardized agriculture. The evils of this lack of credit organization have been greatly exaggerated, but the time has probably come for more organization. . . ." *Ibid.*, p. 745.

uation when it suggested that there be devised a method of cooperative credit through which the farmers could more easily secure loans on fair terms. The report of Senator Aldrich's National Monetary Commission contributed further to the same cause by presenting a favorable account of the German *Landschaft* system of farm-mortgage credit.[61] In addition, in 1912, President Taft called attention to the problem by asking the American ambassadors in Europe to investigate the cooperative credit systems in the countries to which they were assigned.

Perhaps more important than all this was the work of an investigating committee sent to Europe in 1912. In April of that year, the Southern Commercial Congress, mainly through the influence of David Lubin, eminent California agriculturalist, devoted a large share of its program to the rural-credits question. After some discussion the congress authorized "a commission of 70 delegates, representing 29 States and 4 Provinces of Canada," to visit Europe and report upon the cooperative credit systems there in use. This commission was joined by a congressional commission of seven set up in order to make a similar investigation. The result of their combined efforts was a joint report, but the congressional group carried its mandate a step further by submitting a draft of a proposed rural-credit bill based on the *Landschaft* system that had been operating in Germany for over a century and had been adopted more or less by England, France, and other European countries. The extent to which cooperative credit facilities had become a popular goal can be measured by the fact that in the campaign of 1912 the three principal political parties all gave this subject favorable mention in their platforms.[62]

Meanwhile, congressmen, eager to satisfy the demands of their constituents, had flooded the Sixty-third Congress with no less than seventy rural-credit measures. These proposals did not necessarily reflect the acceptance of European precedents; according to one authority, "when

61. James B. Morman, *Farm Credits in the United States and Canada* (New York, 1924), pp. 76–77.
62. Myers, *Cooperative Farm Mortgage Credit*, pp. 5–6. See also the preface of Myron T. Herrick's *Rural Credits, Land and Coöperative* (New York, 1915). Herrick discusses the German *Landschaften* in Chapters 5 to 9. Another study is found in Henry W. Wolff, *Co-operative Credit for the United States* (New York, 1917). See also Pope, in *Quarterly Journal of Economics*, XXVIII (August, 1914), p. 728–29, for a criticism of the commission investigation on European rural credits.

one studies the measures in detail he discovers that instead of profiting by the experience of Europeans our legislators have proposed measures which these have avoided or abandoned." The measures introduced were varied in the extreme. One bill advocated that the national government make direct loans to farmers from funds obtained by the sale of government bonds. Another, assuming that farmers were in no position to conduct their own banking business, asked for the organization of land banks by would-be lenders, who could secure funds by selling the bonds of the banks. A third theory, the one brought back by the American commission, recommended the establishment of cooperative groups of farmer-borrowers who, through their associations, could secure loans from land banks deriving their original capital from the United States government. So marked were the differences, particularly over the last two proposals, that the whole matter had to be turned over to a joint subcommittee on rural credits, composed of members from both houses of Congress. The result of their deliberations was a compromise measure, known as the Federal Farm Loan Act, which became law on July 17, 1916. This law provided two types of rural credits. One was to be furnished by a system of Federal Land Banks, from which loans could be obtained only through cooperative farm-loan associations organized by borrowers; the other, by privately owned joint-stock land banks which could deal directly with individuals in need of funds.[63]

During the period of agricultural expansion that accompanied the participation of the United States in the first World War, the farmers of the nation thus had the advantage of excellent marketing cooperatives for dairy products, grain, and livestock, and a system of rural credits, based mainly on the cooperative principle. These developments may account in some measure for the success with which the farmers met the excessive demands made on them by the war; and they may also explain in part the land boom of the western Middle West that followed the war and the disastrous collapse which it suffered.

63. Myers, *Cooperative Farm Mortgage Credit,* pp. 5–6. Ruth V. Corbin, "Federal Rural Credits, 1916–1936" (unpublished master's thesis, University of Wisconsin, 1936), sheds much light on this general subject.

Chapter IV

THE IMPACT OF WAR

CERTAINLY no other section of the United States was less prepared than the Middle West for the news in August, 1914, that a general war had broken out in Europe. Nor was any section more convinced that the war was strictly Europe's war and not America's. Country dwellers from Chicago westward, while dependent to a degree on world markets for the disposal of their produce, knew little of what went on outside the United States and cared even less. Not a few of them, indeed, had migrated from the Old World to the New to get away from the turmoil and strife of Europe, with its emphasis on universal military training and its constant talk of war. No more convinced isolationists existed anywhere in America than these adopted sons and daughters and their descendants. Later, in opposing the entrance of the United States into the war, they were often less concerned about fighting against the nation of their origin than about having to fight at all. They thought that in migrating to America they had left all that behind.[1]

In commenting on the travail of Europe, *Wallaces' Farmer,* which well represented rural opinion in the Middle West, urged its readers not to take sides, but suggested at the same time that they make ready "to feed the nations." There was no thought that this American contribution would be a free offering; rather it was assumed that war trade would

1. Benton H. Wilcox, "A Reconsideration of the Character and Economic Basis Northwestern Radicalism" (unpublished doctoral dissertation, University of Wisconsin, 1933), p. 139; *Wallaces' Farmer,* XXXIX (August 28, 1914), p. 1165.

bring American producers high profits. Reflecting smugly on the wisdom of Woodrow Wilson's policy of neutrality, the same journal held that the United States should take full advantage of the opportunity presented by the war to promote its national self-sufficiency; not only in agriculture but in industry and commerce as well the American nation should so fully develop its resources that in the future it would "be comparatively untouched by any like manifestation of madness and folly hereafter in any part of the world."[2]

The transition from a determined neutrality to a reluctant acceptance of the necessity for American intervention was made gradually and in some cases without full realization that it was being made at all. For a time middle western farmers seemed almost to ignore the fact that their new prosperity was due primarily to the war. They took comfort in the knowledge that the British navy would control the seas and so insure them a market for everything they could grow, but they overlooked the obvious inference that their incomes were closely linked with the continued successes of Allied sea power. They lauded neutrality, defended unpreparedness, and asserted insistently that the United States must keep out of the war at all costs. A few of them were even strongly pro-German and criticized freely the increasing favoritism for Great Britain and her allies shown by the American government.[3]

But at length the light began to dawn. When, in the spring of 1916 Wilson threatened to break diplomatic relations with Germany, *Wallaces Farmer* inquired, "What hope is there for peace on earth if nations do not consider themselves bound by treaties they have signed, and by the international laws they have helped to make?"[4] By that time the same journal could face the added possibility that the United States would have to protect itself "by force of arms against all comers." Before the end of the year it had even begun to fear that Germany, in spite of her promise to Wilson, might reopen the submarine blockade. To Americans, no less than to Britons, it was now as plain as day that this would be a disaster of the first magnitude. Thus the involvement of the United States in the

2. *Ibid.* (September 25, 1914), p. 1284; (October 9, 1914), p. 1340.
3. *Ibid.* (September 11, 1914), p. 1221; XL (January 1, 1915), pp. 4-5; (June 1915), p. 840; (October 8, 1915), p. 1316.
4. *Ibid.*, XLI (April 28, 1916), p. 664.

war, when it came, was by no means unanticipated. A few middle western farmers raised their voices in protest, but for the most part, like the editor of *Wallaces' Farmer,* they went along with the administration's policy. No doubt they believed at the beginning, as many others did also, that the United States could take the war comfortably, contributing only such naval activity as might be necessary to keep the sea lanes open. But eventually they left their pacificism and isolationism far behind.[5]

The role of producing whatever extra foodstuffs were needed by the fighting powers was accepted by American farmers without hesitation. The United States, wrote the editor of *Wallaces' Farmer,* must accept the "moral responsibility to feed the hungry people of the world."[6] Producers soon learned, however, that in time of war staple commodities such as wheat, livestock, and livestock products were in greatest demand, while such semiluxury foods as fresh fruits and vegetables tended to be forgotten. Furthermore, Great Britain needed American aid to overcome shortages arising from the wartime curtailment of her purchases from continental Europe. The British, for example, had depended a great deal on Denmark and the Netherlands for fats, but lack of feed for livestock in those countries, together with the grave hazards of overseas trade, kept shipments across the North Sea at a minimum. Likewise, the closing of the Dardanelles left the British short of Russian wheat. American farmers cheerfully did their best to make up all such deficits.

Probably the coming of the war had an even greater effect upon American agriculture than was generally recognized. In the three or four years immediately preceding 1914, food production had begun to catch up with the abnormal demands of urbanization. As a result, farm prices were leveling off, and, had there been no war, the price curve would probably have soon turned sharply downward. But the tremendous demands of war changed the situation completely. While the total volume of production soared sharply upward, achieving within a few years levels that might not have been reached for a generation in time of peace, prices not only tended to keep pace with production but in some cases to run far ahead. Also, drastic changes occurred in the American economy as the demands of war diverted farmers from their normal habits into new and more or

5. *Ibid.,* XLII (February 9, 1917), p. 236; (March 30, 1917), p. 564.
6. *Ibid.* (April 6, 1917), p. 604.

less unanticipated activities. Now and then a warning voice pointed out the dangers of such fundamental changes to meet a merely temporary emergency, but for the most part the food producers of America acted as if the changes made during the war would be permanent and gave little thought to the complications that were sure to arise when peace was restored.[7]

The entrance of the United States into the war speeded up tremendously the already abnormal demand for intensive food production. Assured by official propaganda that food would "win the war," farmers planted maximum crops and even brought into production much marginal or semi-marginal land—land that in normal times would not have been worked at all. According to one estimate, not fewer than 45,000,000 acres of new land were so opened up during the war decade. The policy of the government was to stimulate production, regardless of the consequences. With only a few exceptions, prices were allowed to rise in response to the pyramiding demand, and in addition to the incentive of high prices government pamphleteers and publicists bombarded the farmers with appeals for greater production on patriotic grounds. With reasonably good weather conditions and the certainty of inflated prices, production went up amazingly. The average annual value of the American farm output from 1910 to 1914 was about six billion dollars, but by 1917 the take was thirteen billions, over fourteen billions by 1918, and nearly sixteen billions by 1919. For a year and a half after the end of the war the wave of farm prosperity continued. The obligation to feed the Allies had ceased, but the demands of war-ravaged Europe for American foodstuffs continued. And the productive powers of the American farmer remained intact.[8]

The greatest single crop demand on the United States was for wheat. In a sense this was nothing new, for heavy wheat shipments from the United States to Europe, particularly to England, were normal. Since the

7. A. B. Genung, "Agriculture in the World War Period," U. S. Dept. Agr. Yearbook, *Farmers in a Changing World* (Washington, 1940), pp. 278–80.

8. E. T. Meredith, "Report of the Secretary of Agriculture," U. S. Dept. Agr. *Yearbook,* 1916, p. 17; G. E. Mowry, "The Decline of Agriculture, 1920–1924, Study in Economics and Politics" (unpublished master's thesis, University of Wisconsin, 1934), p. 6; Edwin G. Nourse, *Government in Relation to Agriculture* (Washington, 1940), p. 879; *Wallaces' Farmer,* XLII (April 6, 1917), p. 604.

British economy was geared to manufacturing rather than to agriculture, Great Britain had long imported greater quantities of wheat than did any other nation in the world. The leading port of entry for this commodity was Liverpool, and for years the Liverpool price of wheat had been recognized as the governing price for wheat, wherever it might be sold. Most of Great Britain's agricultural land had long since been turned into meadows and pasture, with possibly as little as 3 per cent of it in use for the growing of bread grains. After the war began, when the Russian wheat supply was cut off, there was much plowing up of ancient pastures —some of them hundreds of years old—and much replanting, but the main source of grain supply continued to be importation, principally from the United States, Canada, and the Argentine. Heavy British buying on the American market shot wheat prices upward with incredible speed. The wildest day ever witnessed on the Chicago exchange was the day that war was declared in Europe. By December, 1914, wheat was bringing about twenty-three cents per bushel more than at the same time the preceding year, and in spite of a bumper crop—Kansas alone harvested in 1914 almost twice as much wheat as the state had ever grown before— wheat prices continued to soar. By the spring of 1915 farmers at interior points were getting as high as $1.25 to $1.40 per bushel for all the wheat they could supply, and wheat exports from the United States were running to about $55,000,000 per month.[9]

The heavy demand and the high prices led naturally to a great expansion of wheat sowing in the fall of 1914 and the spring of 1915. During the decade that had preceded the war, the average annual acreage devoted to the growing of wheat had been about 48,000,000 acres, of which 30,000,000 had been in winter wheat and 18,000,000 in spring wheat. In the fall of 1914 the area sown to winter wheat was expanded by 5,000,000 acres, while in the spring of 1915 another extra 2,000,000 acres were sown to spring wheat. During the year 1915 over 60,000,000 acres of wheat were harvested, with a yield per acre that was phenomenally high. That year the United States produced more than a billion bushels of wheat, the greatest yield ever recorded up to that time and for many years to come.

9. *Ibid.*, XXXIX (August 14, 1914), p. 1110; (September 11, 1914), p. 1244; October 16, 1914), p. 1496; (December 11, 1914), p. 1614; XLII (January 26, 1917), 138; Genung, in *Farmers in a Changing World*, p. 281.

Approximately one-fourth of this crop was sent abroad. So bountiful was the 1915 yield, not only in the United States but also throughout the world, that the price of wheat dropped to the prewar level of less than a dollar a bushel and remained low until the spring of 1916.[10]

Naturally this slump in price affected the acreage devoted to wheat in 1916. That year only 52,000,000 acres of wheat were harvested, and the yield—partly because of an epidemic of black rust—dropped to 636,000,000 bushels. But the war demands continued, and the price responded. By December, 1916, wheat was bringing the American farmer $1.60 a bushel, and predictions were made that if there should be another short crop the price would rise to $3.00. The effect of German resumption of submarine warfare early in 1917 caused a tremendous break in most American prices, including wheat, which dropped as much as fifteen cents a bushel; but the drop was not to last.[11] By April 1 wheat was up to $1.80, and following the entrance of the United States into the war a few days later, the rise was precipitate. Early in May, 1917, cash wheat touched the fantastic figure of $3.48 a bushel. It should be noted, however, that this sudden rise in price netted the actual dirt farmer very little, since at the time it occurred most available grain was already in the hands of speculators and distributors.[12]

The 1917 wheat yield was little or no better than that of 1916. Under authority of a sweeping Food Control Act, signed on August 10, 1917, the President set $2.20 as the minimum price for the 1917 crop. The law itself set a price of $2.00 a bushel on wheat for the 1918 crop, but gave the President authority to guarantee for a period not to exceed eighteen months whatever price he deemed necessary to ensure producers a reasonable profit. It was under the terms of this act that Herbert Hoover became Food Administrator and devoted himself assiduously to the encouragement of food production. But neither legislation nor presidential price

10. *Ibid.,* pp. 280–81.

11. *Ibid.,* pp. 281–84; *Wallaces' Farmer,* XL (July 9, 1915), p. 960; (November 12, 1915), p. 1505; XLII (February 9, 1917), p. 236; (May 25, 1917), p. 836; (August 3, 1917), p. 1096.

12. F. M. Surface, *The Stabilization of the Price of Wheat During the War and its Effect upon the Returns to the Producer* (Washington, 1925), p. 12; B. H. Hibbard, *Effects of the Great War upon Agriculture in the United States and Great Britain* (New York, 1919), p. 27.

fixing could control the weather, and the total harvest for the year was almost exactly the same as for 1916—only 650,828,000 bushels. Price fixing had come too late to ensure for all the crop the high return which the President had set. Estimates made by the Department of Agriculture indicate that the average price per bushel actually received by the American producer for his wheat in 1917 was $1.44.[13]

As noted, the Food Administration Act of 1917 set a minimum price of $2.00 per bushel for the 1918 crop in the hope that such a guaranteed high price would ensure the bountiful yield that the Allied war effort so greatly needed. The low yield of 1917 held American exports down to 138,000,000 bushels, and that figure was made possible only by the most drastic economies at home. In 1918 crop conditions were better, and the President, on June 21, 1918, used the authority given him in the Food Control Act to raise the minimum price, this time to $2.26. The net result was a harvest of 921,000,000 bushels, less by far than the bumper yield of 1915 but still a phenomenally high figure. Of this crop, 287,000,000 bushels were shipped overseas.[14]

Although the fighting part of the war came to an end officially with the armistice of November 11, 1918, the European demand for American wheat continued strong throughout 1919, and the government of the United States maintained its price guarantee to the farmers. As a result, the wheat sown was about 75,000,000 acres—the highest in all American history—and the yield came to more than 967,000,000 bushels. Of this crop about 220,000,000 bushels were exported. Strangely enough, the American farmer assumed that the wartime expansion of his wheat market abroad would continue indefinitely and made little effort to curtail production, either by abandoning marginal land or by shifting to other crops. In consequence, the wheat yield of 1920 was 833,000,000 bushels, a figure that was approximated, more or less, each year throughout the next decade. But neither the wartime market nor the European demand which had helped to sustain it continued long after the war. Furthermore, at midnight on May 31, 1920, the government guarantee on the

13. *Ibid.*, p. 29; Simon Litman, *Prices and Price Control in Great Britain and the United States during the World War* (New York, 1920), pp. 207-9, 219-21.
14. Surface, *Stabilization of the Price of Wheat*, p. 17; Genung, in *Farmers in a Changing World*, pp. 282-83.

price of wheat was removed and wheat dropped precipitately, thus laying among wheat farmers firm foundations for an era of discontent.[15]

The wartime boom in wheat was paralleled closely by a similar expansion of the corn-livestock industry. The heaviest items of meat export from the United States to Europe, both before and during the war, were pork and pork products, especially lard. With regard to these items the same as with wheat, the war did not so much serve to open up a new type of market for American produce abroad as to accentuate an already existing market. About 12 per cent of American pork and pork products had been shipped overseas in the prewar years, and during the war this proportion was approximately doubled. The average lard export from the United States to Great Britain during the five prewar years was about 450,000,000 pounds; by 1919 it was over a billion pounds.[16]

The effect of the acute wartime demand upon livestock producers was in most respects similar to its effect on the growers of wheat. But there were differences. A constant factor in the livestock industry that had no parallel in the wheat industry was the relation between the price of corn and the price of livestock, particularly hogs. If the price of corn rose more rapidly than the price of hogs, the tendency was for the farmer to sell his hogs rather than to buy expensive corn to fatten them. Corn prices were affected not only by the demand for feed, but also by the size and quality of the corn crop in a given year and by the export demand, which shot up considerably during the war period. Principally because of two bad years, 1916 and 1918, corn production during the war showed practically no increase over prewar years. There was some importation of Argentine corn, but this was more than offset by wartime exportation to Europe. As a result of these various factors, corn prices tended, from the feeders' point of view, to be abnormally high in proportion to the price obtainable for hogs. In the fall of 1914, for example, corn sold for nearly seventy-five cents a bushel, much too high a price to justify feeding it to hogs, which were then selling at the comparatively low price of about $8.00 per hundredweight. According to a well-established rule-of-thumb ratio current

15. *Ibid.*, pp. 283; *Statistical Abstract of the United States, 1923*, p. 181; F. M Surface, *The Grain Trade during the World War* (New York, 1928), p. 459; E. G Nourse, *American Agriculture and the European Market* (New York, 1924), p. 79
16. Genung, in *Farmers in a Changing World*, pp. 286–87.

in farmer circles, for each hundred pounds of hog the producer should receive thirteen or fourteen times the average cost per bushel of the corn fed to the hogs. Hence, with seventy-five-cent corn, the price of hogs should have been not less than $9.75 per hundredweight rather than $8.00. One curious result of this imbalance was that more and more hogs were thrown on the market, thus keeping the hog price down.[17]

By the year 1916 the hog price had begun to rise, but the amount of pork and pork products available for shipment overseas was not nearly enough to supply the demand. With the entrance of the United States into the war and the creation of the Food Administration, every effort was made to remedy this situation. The Food Administration, however, made no attempt to fix livestock prices in a manner as forthright as it used in pegging the price of wheat. What it did instead was to enlist the cooperation of the middlemen. In this way it sought to assure a price of $15.50 per hundredweight for hogs, and to manipulate the corn-hog ratio in such fashion that the farmer would be ensured thirteen times the average cost per bushel of the corn fed into the hogs for each hundred pounds of hog ready for market. In the fall of 1917 the Chicago Board of Trade put a maximum price of $1.28 on all future deliveries of corn and refused to permit a higher price to be quoted.[18]

While the Food Administration found it impracticable to maintain the thirteen-to-one ratio, it did succeed in keeping hog prices at a reasonably high figure. In the fall of 1917 hogs averaged about $15 per hundredweight; by September, 1918, they reached $17.50; and by the summer of 1919 they stood at over $19. Although this was less than the farmers claimed they needed, it was enough to stimulate production. Exports of lard in 1917 had actually dropped below the figure for the year before, but in 1918 they rose by more than 47 per cent, and in 1919 by nearly 39 per cent more. Exports of such pork products as bacon, ham, and shoulders showed similar enormous gains. Here again the way was paved for a

17. *Ibid.*, p. 284; *Statistical Abstract of the United States*, 1920, p. 146; *Wallaces' Farmer*, XXXIX (September 18, 1914), p. 1256; XL (March 19, 1915), p. 480; XLI (February 25, 1916), p. 310; XLIII (April 12, 1918), p. 640; (October 11, 1918), p. 1466.

18. Genung, in *Farmers in a Changing World*, p. 286; *Wallaces' Farmer*, XLIII (March 15, 1918), pp. 484–85.

terrific collapse after the war, whenever the foreign demand for American supplies returned to normal.[19]

The beef cattle story repeats the corn-hog story with variations. Most important of the differences was the fact that the Argentine, rather than the United States, had been the chief source of supply for Europe before the war and no doubt would have continued in that capacity during the war but for the shipping shortage. With shipping at a premium, however, as the war wore on the short trip across the North Atlantic tended to overbalance the higher cost of United States beef, so that American exports of this commodity grew by leaps and bounds. Whereas total exports of beef from the United States had reached only 150,000,000 pounds in 1914, four years later the figure was 954,000,000. The increase in beef production necessary to make these figures possible was not accomplished without earnest effort. Beef cattle require pasture, and the tendency of the times, as already noted, was to plow up pastures and meadows, even in regions of inadequate rainfall, in order to plant wheat or other grain. Moreover, although Americans patriotically ate less pork during the war, their consumption of beef actually showed a per capita increase.[20]

While the Food Administration neither made a price guarantee, as in the case of wheat, nor designated a fair price, as with hogs, it did promise to do its best to see that the cattle growers were adequately remunerated. In its efforts to support the market, however, the Food Administration had always to keep an eye on the American consumer, whose cries of anguish as prices rose had strong political repercussions. Farmers claimed that in response to consumer protests the Food Administration actually urged the packers to keep their prices down, much to the disadvantage of the producer. Actually, beef prices advanced from an average of $6.24 in 1914 to $9.56 in 1919, while at the end of the war superior beef-steer cattle brought as high as $17.50 per hundredweight on the Chicago market. So stimulated, the cattle industry expanded in spite of all obstacles. When the war ended the number of beef cattle owned by American farmers had increased by 20 per cent. Just what was to happen when

19. Hibbard, *Effects of the Great War upon Agriculture*, p. 132; *Statistical Abstract of the United States*, 1920, p. 497.

20. Genung, in *Farmers in a Changing World*, pp. 287–88; *Wallaces' Farmer* XLIII (March 22, 1918), p. 539; XLIV (April 11, 1919), p. 853.

the normal flow of beef from the Argentine to Europe began again, few seemed to consider.[21]

The dairy industry was in general less disturbed by the war than other major farm activities in the western Middle West. The first serious impact of war upon dairy farmers came during the years 1915 and 1916, when the price of milk failed to rise along with those of other commodities. Since the cost of producing milk had risen with the higher prices that had to be paid for feed and labor, the dairy farmers soon found themselves well along the road to bankruptcy. For this situation they blamed the distributors of milk, especially those in such metropolitan areas as Chicago and Des Moines, whom the farmers accused of setting prices regardless of the effect on the producers. Made desperate by this situation, some dairy farmers sold their cows and got out of business, but others made use of existing milk-producers' associations to force a rise in the price of milk. A climax was reached late in October, 1917, when the Milk Producers' Association, an organization of about 16,000 dairy farmers, threatened to stop the shipment of milk into the Chicago market unless the demand of the producers for $3.42 per hundred pounds was met. At this point the state food administrator decided to intervene by appointing an arbitration commission whose job it was to name the price to be paid the producer. This price was to be based on the cost of production plus a reasonable profit to the producer and the cost of distribution plus a reasonable profit to the distributor. Pending an investigation the producer was to accept $3.22 per hundred and the distributor was to retail it at 12 cents a quart. An agreement relative to price was reached only after a mass of data had been compiled on feed and labor costs. The prices per hundredweight first agreed upon to be paid the dairy farmers in 1918 were: February, $3.07; March, $2.83; April, $2.49; May, $2.04; June, $1.80. After further discussions the price to be paid for milk in March was raised from $2.83 to $3.10 per hundred, and the prices to be paid during the following months were to be based on figures published by the United States Department of Agriculture.[22]

21. Genung, in *Farmers in a Changing World*, p. 287.
22. Hibbard, *Effects of the Great War upon Agriculture*, pp. 136–45; *Wallaces' Farmer*, XLI (April 21, 1916), p. 633; XLII (August 10, 1917), p. 1104; (October 12, 1917), p. 1376; XLIII (May 24, 1918), p. 848; (August 2, 1918), p. 1104; XLIV

Eventually, particularly toward the end of the war, the prices of dairy products increased substantially, although in the case of milk and butter-fat never in comparable degree with the prices of feedstuffs. By 1918 dairy products had registered an average increase of 70 per cent, while the farm price of butter had risen from 25 cents at the beginning of the war to 54 cents at its close. Even the high price of butter did not serve to keep up butter production, which declined during the last two years of the war in spite of heavy exports—34,000,000 pounds in 1919, compared with an average of 4,250,000 pounds in the five prewar years. Butter exports, however, were small in comparison with total production; only 2 per cent of the American output was sent overseas. Most important of the dairy industry products from the export point of view were cheese and evaporated milk. The demand for American cheese abroad increased the total export of that item during the war from an initial 1 per cent of the total amount manufactured to a final 12 per cent. Evaporated milk by the end of the war was exported to the extent of 853,000,000 pounds, nearly half the total produced in the United States and nearly fifty times the prewar export figures. Thus the dairy industry, whatever the complaints of the milk producers, was given a real lift by the war. The number of milk cows on farms increased during the war more than 8.5 per cent, and the total output of cheese, butter, and evaporated milk more than 7 per cent. As long as the high wartime wages lasted, the city population could and did buy milk and other dairy products in far greater amounts than formerly. But obviously dairy farming, while expanded by the war, was not overexpanded in like degree with the wheat, corn, and livestock industries. To the milk producers, the collapse of the boom, when it came, would therefore be less distressing.[23]

The farmers of the western Middle West, whose interests lay primarily in the production of these basic foodstuffs, undoubtedly took a heavy profit out of the war. Never before had American farmers received such prices. Yet they did not think of themselves as profiteers. One authority reported that from the 1917 crop the average farmer received not more than from seventy-five cents to a dollar an hour for his labor, while the 1918 crop

(April 25, 1919), p. 944; (May 16, 1919), p. 1065; Litman, *Prices and Price Control*, pp. 256–59.

23. *Ibid.*, pp. 190, 256–61; Genung, in *Farmers in a Changing World*, p. 288.

because of his mounting expenses, netted him even less. Indeed, the farmers sometimes felt that they had a grievance, for the government had exerted its authority by intervening directly to control the price of wheat and indirectly to keep down the prices of hogs and other agricultural products. The cost-plus method—applied so generously to packers, shipbuilders, and contractors—had not been made available to the farmers. Nor was there any way to figure the loss in fertility that came from plowing up land to expand grain growing nor the damage done by short-term tenants, whose wasteful methods greatly depreciated the value of the farms they exploited. *Wallaces' Farmer,* fascinated by the cost-of-production problem on the farm, figured that the average cost per acre to produce a field of corn was $19 in 1917 and $23 in 1918, whereas during the period 1897 to 1906 it had been $10. Good farmers might spend as much as $40 an acre on their corn. All this was very well if the price was high enough and the yield was good, but at best the farmer took grave risks. The same journal held that western farmers who had made a profit of $18 per acre on their corn in 1917 probably made not more than $9 per acre on the 1918 crop, and the next year even less. As for net returns per hour of labor, the following calculations, while by no means entirely dependable, give some idea of what the farmer thought he was making.[24]

NET RETURNS PER HOUR OF LABOR[25]

	Iowa		North Central States	
	1917	*1918*	*1917*	*1918*
Corn	.98	.88	.92	.52
Wheat	1.26	1.08	.88	1.00
Oats	1.10	.58	.98	.68
Rye	.93	.77	.84	.40
Barley	1.63	.58	.72	.23
Potatoes	1.11	.44	.85	.65
Hay	.13	− .60	.77	− .05

Although most farmers seemingly failed to see the breakers ahead, a few warning voices were raised. The editor of *Wallaces' Farmer* repeatedly pointed out that prices were bound to drop at the close of the war and

24. *Wallaces' Farmer,* XLIII (November 29, 1918), p. 1741; (December 27, 1918), p. 1891; XLIV (March 14, 1919), p. 660.
25. *Ibid.,* XLIII (December 27, 1918), p. 1891.

urged the farmers to plan accordingly. If the descent down the price ladder could be made "a rung at a time," this sagacious observer was sure that all would be well. Otherwise, he feared, "someone will get pushed off." High war wages for labor, together with high prices for manufactured goods and high prices for agricultural produce, he argued, must all come down together. Certainly the farmer ought not to bear the first full brunt of price reductions all alone. In actual fact, except for a flurry of excitement at the time of the unexpectedly early armistice, prices remained good on most farm commodities throughout 1919 and on into 1920. The price of wheat was supported by law until May 31, 1920, but such guarantees as were given on hog prices were removed in the spring of 1919 without a serious price break. Hog prices averaged over $18 per hundredweight throughout the year 1919 and $14 in 1920. But by 1921 the average was only a little over $8.[26]

By this time the boom was over and the long depression in agriculture had begun. Beginning slowly in June, hard on the disappearance of the government guarantee on wheat, the descent down the price ladder gathered momentum as the season's abundant crops poured on the market. By November 1, 1920, farm prices were 33 per cent lower than the level of the previous year; by the next midsummer, they were down 85 per cent. On the other hand, the prices of what the farmer had to buy showed no such changes. According to one estimate, a given volume of farm produce would buy only 75 per cent as much in 1921 as it would in 1914. Individual items showed an even greater disparity. In 1919 one-fifth of a bushel of corn would buy a gallon of gasoline, but in 1921 the price equivalent was two bushels of corn. In 1919 six bushels of corn would buy a ton of coal, but in 1921 it took sixty bushels. The average price paid to the Nebraska producer for his corn in November, 1921, was twenty-five cents a bushel and prices as low as eleven cents were on record. Under these circumstances it was cheaper to burn corn for fuel than to buy coal, and many farmers did exactly that. Throughout the twenties and on into the thirties the farmers' travail continued. Rural standards of living went down, and many farmers, either from choice or from necessity, gave up

26. *Ibid.*, XLIV (January 17, 1919), p. 112; (January 24, 1919), p. 185; (March 14, 1919), p. 701; *Statistical Abstract of the United States*, 1923, p. 163.

the struggle. According to one estimate, the actual number of farms and farmers was reduced during these years by a million.[27]

Probably the factor which contributed more than any other to the deepness of this depression was the land boom that had accompanied the war prices. It was natural for the farmer, with a high income for almost the first time in his life, to pay off his debts, buy new machinery, improve his property, acquire automobiles, victrolas, and other articles he had long coveted. But it was a temptation, also, to buy more land, both as a means of increasing his profits and as a means of acquiring greater wealth by speculation. When new acquisitions, whether of land or of other property, were paid for in full, the chance of catastrophe was not so great. But when, as was so often the case, the purchases were financed in part by mortgages or made on the installment plan, the purchaser was merely gambling on the continuance of high prices. Some land transactions were the sheerest speculation, with down payments comparable to the smallest margins of stock market operations in 1929. According to an Iowa observer, "Half of the people here are either land agents or speculators in land. Most of the men have never been farmers, and never will be farmers. The game is to buy and sell, and many are boasting of making thirty and forty thousand dollars in a few months. And then they say the boom is just started."[28] Nearly 95 per cent of the land buyers in Iowa paid down in cash only 10 per cent or less, and nearly three-fourths of them paid only 5 per cent or less. The initial payment, however, was merely to bind the sale, and approximately one-third of the purchase price was normally expected by the next March 1, the date usually set for giving possession to a farm. Some farmers who sold out retired to live on their fortunes; others

27. Henry C. Wallace, "The Year in Agriculture," U. S. Dept. Agri., Yearbook, 1920, pp. 17–18; Archibald MacDonald McIsaac, "Whither Agriculture?" in J. G. Smith, ed., Facing the Facts: An Economic Diagnosis (New York, 1932), p. 290; F. M. Surface, American Food in the World War and Reconstruction Period (Stanford, Calif., 1931), p. 114; Warren S. Thompson and P. K. Whelpton, Population Trends in the United States (New York, 1937), p. 19; Mowry, "Decline of Agriculture," pp. 16–19.

28. Wallaces' Farmer, XLIV (June 20, 1919), p. 1256. See also Archibald M. Woodruff, Jr., Farm Mortgage Loans of Life Insurance Companies (New Haven, Conn., 1937), pp. 19–23; E. R. A. Seligman, The Economics of Farm Relief (New York, 1929), pp. 15–16.

bought more land, not only for themselves but sometimes also for their sons.[29]

Land prices began to rise as early as 1915 and continued the upward spiral until 1920. For the country as a whole, the price of land was up 40 per cent by the end of the year 1918 and up 70 per cent by the end of 1919, the worst year of the boom. Corn land, especially in Iowa and Illinois, made the most fantastic advances. In the former state the average price per acre had been $82.58 in 1910, but by 1920 it was $199.52; in Illinois during the same period, the rise was from $95.02 to $164.20.[30] Many individual purchases quite exceeded these figures. "Iowans believe," wrote one optimist in 1919, "that land is going higher, and that it can never be bought cheaper than at present. They buy therefore to avoid paying a higher price later on. They say there is but one corn belt to grow corn and hogs and the demand for these products is increasing and will continue to increase."[31] Inspired by such beliefs, purchasers paid as high as $300 or $400 an acre for some Iowa land and occasionally even $500. "Experts" were available to defend such prices as entirely reasonable. They maintained, with fair plausibility, that the price of land had been going up ever since the disappearance of the frontier and was bound to go up further. Corn land, they claimed, had risen during the past about $2 per acre for every cent of increase in the price of corn. Thus, in 1890 when corn brought 20 cents a bushel, corn land had sold for $30 an acre; in 1913, when corn brought 55 cents a bushel, the land that produced it had sold for $100 an acre; hence, they argued, with prices at $1 a bushel, the land should bring $190 per acre.[32]

To a very great extent the land boom, and the farmers' prosperity in general, was financed by rural banks. Loans from the Federal Farm Loan System were available, with rates of interest perhaps .5 per cent lower

29. *Iowa Yearbook of Agriculture,* 1919, p. 582; Woodruff, *Farm Mortgage Loans,* p. 22; L. C. Gray and O. G. Lloyd, *Farm Land Values in Iowa,* U. S. Dept. Agri., Bulletin 874 (Washington, 1920), p. 15.

30. *Statistical Abstract of the United States,* 1923, p. 140.

31. *Iowa Yearbook of Agriculture,* 1919, p. 583.

32. I. W. Wright, *Farm Mortgage Financing* (New York, 1923), pp. 9–13; John D. Black, *Agricultural Reform in the United States* (New York, 1929), p. 21; Freida Baird and Claude L. Benner, *Ten Years of Federal Intermediate Credits* (Washington, 1933), p. 29.

than had been customary before its advent and with the longer period
for amortization of the loan. Life insurance companies also had an abundance of money on hand for real estate loans. But the local small-town
bankers, many with huge surplus deposits that they were eager to put to
work, literally pressed money upon the not unwilling farmers and speculators. New banks were established by men who knew next to nothing
about banking, often by retired farmers with their wartime profits as
capital. From 1914 to 1920 more than 1,700 new banks began operations
in eleven typical agricultural states. Often two or three banks appeared
where one would have been enough.[33]

With money from so many sources so easily obtainable, the farmers of
the boom-stricken area were tempted further and further into debt. Mortgages on farms in the western Middle West increased over 128 per cent
during the decade that ended with the year 1920. According to the United
States Department of Agriculture, in 1915 the banks of the country "had
outstanding to farmers, loans on personal and collateral security to the
amount of $1,609,970,000." By 1918 this figure had grown to $2,506,814,000,
and in 1920 to $3,869,891,000. Much farmer borrowing was for other pur-
poses than to buy land, although all such debts were an ultimate charge
on the land and what it could produce. Farmers who might have paid off
old debts when prices were good often borrowed money in order instead to
gain for themselves the living standards of city dwellers. More and more,
the farmers bought washing machines, electric sweepers, radios, and automobiles. They sent their children to college. They improved their houses
and built new ones. To the rural bankers, loans for all such items seemed
reasonable and the cash was in the till or could easily be obtained from
the Federal Reserve Banks. Few seemed to realize that a change in policy
on the part of the Federal Reserve System might easily dry up the farmers'
credit or to understand the problems inherent in such an eventuality.[34]

Both farmers and bankers should have known that the spending spree
could not last forever. The high valuations set on farm land were not in

33. *Ibid.*, pp. 25–26; *Wallaces' Farmer*, XLIV (May 16, 1919), p. 1064; Wood-
uff, *Farm Mortgage Loans*, pp. 23–24.
34. *Statistical Abstract of the United States*, 1923, p. 146; Black, *Agricultural
Reform*, p. 37; Woodruff, *Farm Mortgage Loans*, pp. 25–29; Baird and Benner,
Ten Years of Federal Intermediate Credits, p. 25.

reality justified by its earning power, even in the years of prosperity. Perhaps an occasional superior farmer might make his farm pay a reasonable percentage on the investment, but the ordinary farmer did well to realize as much as 3 per cent. As a matter of fact, to the great distress of the small-town bankers and the farmers who had borrowed from them, the Federal Reserve Board did reverse the policy of credit expansion that had been standard during the war. In its sixth annual report the board stated its new policy: "The expansion of credit set in motion by the war must be checked. Credit must be brought under effective control and its flow once more regulated and governed with careful regard to the economic welfare of the country and the needs of its producing industries."[35]

Possibly the farmers might have staved off the worst effects of the depression a little longer by additional borrowing, but with this alternative denied them and with the cost of production up and prices down, great numbers of them were obliged to dispose of their land. The high boom prices of real estate came tumbling down. Many who were obliged to sell realized only enough to pay their debts and came out of the ordeal as tenants on the farms they once had owned. Others lost their farms through bankruptcy proceedings. Those who were able to hold on to their land found its value alarmingly diminished. Suppose, for example, a man had purchased a farm for $20,000 during the last year of the boom, with a mortgage of $10,000 on it. By 1928 his farm would have shrunk in value to about $14,000, while the mortgage would probably have remained the same. Thus the farmer's equity would have declined from $10,000 to $4,000. And how could a $4,000 investment support a $10,000 mortgage?[36]

Naturally the collapse of land values fell with devastating effect upon the small-town bankers who had put up the money to back the real estate boom. Too many of these bankers had lent without discrimination, and the so-called "frozen assets" on which they blamed their troubles were in reality practically worthless. Often they had lent to individuals whom they knew to be doubtful risks, and some of them had even ignored sound banking policy by lending altogether too much money to a few favored customers. The epidemic of bank failures began as early as 1920 and continued throughout the decade. The lowest number of such failures came

35. *Ibid.*, pp. 30–31.
36. Black, *Agricultural Reform*, p. 17; Woodruff, *Farm Mortgage Loans*, p. 56

in 1922, with 367 for the country as a whole, and the highest in 1926, when there were no fewer than 976 suspensions, mostly in the small towns and country districts. Aid from the Federal Reserve Banks and other credit sources enabled many bankers to delay the final reckoning for a time, but in an alarmingly large number of cases the collapse could only be postponed. As a result of these failures, many farmers who had resisted the temptation to make speculative land purchases suffered along with the culpable. Some of them lost all of their savings; when they had owned bank stock, they were also subject to heavy assessments that became a lien on their property. Indeed, the general demoralization that inevitably accompanies a series of bank failures left almost no individual in all the Middle West untouched. In the place of the boom psychology that had accompanied and succeeded the war, the whole agricultural population suffered from an atmosphere surcharged with gloom.[37]

The gradual loss of the European wartime markets contributed heavily to this state of mind. Predictions had been common during the war that the food demands of Europe on American producers in the postwar period would greatly exceed the volume of the prewar years. Perhaps the general currency of this idea served to stimulate European production; in any event, European crop yields, at least outside Russia, mounted rapidly after the war came to an end. All the land was still there, even if some of it had been fought over, and its fertility was undiminished. After demobilization there was no longer a labor shortage. With a few simple tools and the will to work, European farmers were soon able to bring the land into full production again. The huge wartime purchases by European governments, paid for with money lent by the United States, were speedily discontinued, and normal trade routes, such as had previously brought so much Argentine beef to Europe, were as speedily resumed. During the war the United Kingdom had imported 50 per cent of its fresh beef from the United States; by 1923 imports from America had fallen to about 5 per cent. Wheat from Canada, the Argentine, and Australia was available for European purchase in ever increasing volume and at discouragingly low prices. European consumers during the war had

37. William Howard Steiner, *Money and Banking* (New York, 1933), pp. 275, 283; Fred L. Garlock, "Bank Failures in Iowa," *Journal of Land and Public Utility Economics,* II (January, 1926), pp. 48–66.

learned to eat less or differently, and the per capita consumption of some staples after the war refused to rise. Strained credit relations, mounting tariff barriers, and the almost universal aim among nations for economic self-sufficiency—each played a part in holding American exports to Europe at a minimum.[38]

Nor was the American market all that it might have been. The per capita consumption of cereals in the United States, with the exception of rice, had long been on the decline. During the first quarter of the twentieth century the consumption of wheat flour had diminished by 20 per cent; corn meal over 60 per cent; rye flour about 60 per cent; and barley, which had been used chiefly in the manufacture of beer, nearly 90 per cent. The eating habits of the people seemed in some respects to be permanently changed by the war, although there was probably little or no actual decline in calorie consumption. With many the substitution of other foods for bread and meat—"Hooverizing"—had become a habit. Restrictions on the use of wheat flour were lifted by 1919, but public eating places did not always return to the practices of serving extra slices of bread free of charge, nor housewives to their earlier recipes. The per capita consumption of meat and meat products had likewise declined, although after the war ended there was a considerable rise in the use of pork and milk. Sugar, and to a lesser degree vegetables, also showed increases. For this condition inflationary prices—the high cost of living—bore some responsibility; so also did the brief industrial depression of the early twenties which, while it lasted, seriously curbed the purchasing power of city laborers. Dieting, particularly by women interested in achieving more stream-lined figures, was sometimes blamed, but could hardly have had much effect. Altogether, according to one economist, "Instead of population pressing upon food supply, food supply is pressing upon population."[39]

The American farmer had other troubles in addition to a limited market. Taxes continued to rise at an alarming rate all through the postwar decade. For the country as a whole the farmer in 1913 had paid 55 cents

38. C. A. Wiley, *Agriculture and the Business Cycle* (Madison, Wis., 1930) pp. 128, 168–78; Nourse, *Government in Relation to Agriculture*, pp. 881–82.

39. O. E. Baker, "Changes in Production and Consumption of our Farm Product and the Trend in Population," *Annals of the American Academy of Political and Social Science,* CXLII (March, 1929), pp. 117, 123, 127, 131; Wiley, *Agriculture and the Business Cycle*, pp. 114–15, 165; Seligman, *Economics of Farm Relief*, p. 24

in taxes for each $100 in real property, but by 1932 he was paying $1.50. From 1913 to 1929 the rise had persisted, year after year, with the single exception of 1918, when there had been a drop from 58 to 57 cents. Real estate values, in terms of the 1913 level, stood at 160 per cent in 1920, 114 per cent in 1929, and 87 per cent in 1932. But taxes in the same years stood at 209 per cent, 241 per cent, and 189 per cent of the 1913 figures. In Iowa alone taxes rose from $96,000,000 in 1920 to $110,000,000 in 1930—a $14,000,000 increase in a decade when prices were going steadily down.[40]

The rising cost of doing business was another headache for the farmer. Farm wages, according to the most trustworthy estimates, had risen from the prewar level by the index figures of 101 in 1914, 239 in 1920, and 170 in 1927, while the prices of the things the farmer had to buy had shown a similar ascending curve. With his earnings down and consumers' goods, equipment, and wages still up, the farmer's struggle to keep solvent grew harder year by year. Transportation costs provided still another heavy item of expense. Freight rates, after two preliminary boosts of 5 per cent and 15 per cent respectively in the region east of the Mississippi and north of the Potomac, were increased by 25 per cent for the country as a whole in 1918. This meant for most of the western Middle West a total increase of about 50 per cent. Still another increase occurred in August, 1920. Meanwhile, although farm prices also had been rising, even faster than the freight rates, the break in prices came just before the last major advance in rates took place. Sharp protests on the part of the rate payers brought from the railroads a voluntary reduction of 10 per cent on the shipment of farm commodities in January, 1922, followed shortly thereafter by a general cut of 10 per cent; but absolutely essential transportation costs still took a formidable share of the farmers' profits.[41]

Numerous necessary readjustments in farming methods made another heavy dent in the farmer's budget. New and expensive machinery was available, and the farmer who lacked it was at a serious disadvantage.

40. *The Farmers' Tax Problem* (73 Congress, 2 session, House Document 406, Serial 10126, Washington, 1934), p. 10; J. O. Babcock, "The Farm Revolt in Iowa," *Social Forces*, XII (March, 1934), p. 369; McIsaac, in *Facing the Facts*, p. 290; G. F. Warren and F. A. Pearson, *The Agricultural Situation* (New York, 1924), p. 32.

41. *Ibid.*, pp. 1–5; J. C. Folsom, "Relief from Farm Labor Costs," *Annals of the American Academy of Political and Social Science*, CXLII (March, 1929), pp. 196–201; H. Gabriel, "Transportation Rates and Facilities," *ibid.*, p. 147.

Horses and mules on many farms, and for that matter in the cities also, were being replaced in considerable part by tractors, trucks, and automobiles. Acreage previously required to raise hay and oats for draft animals was increasingly set free for other purposes. It was estimated in 1929 that not less than twenty million acres had thus been made available for the production of food crops. But the farmer had to buy both the trucks and tractors and the gasoline or kerosene to run them. He also, unless he expanded the number of his cattle and hogs, lost the natural fertilizer that his draft stock had produced and had to depend more and more on expensive commercial fertilizer. Better methods of farming, better breeds of livestock, better types of seed grain, and more attention to diversification—all preached persistently by the Department of Agriculture and the state colleges of agriculture—might bring an increase in agricultural production, but for even his best efforts the farmer seemed to be only worse off financially each suceeding year.[42]

An economist divided the farmers who failed in the postwar depression into four groups.[43] First, there was the farmer, usually a young man, who purchased his land, livestock, and equipment at the high price prevailing during the years 1918 to 1920. He had to pay the penalty for misjudging prices. A second group consisted of farmers who purchased cattle, sheep, and hogs for feeding purposes early in 1920. These farmers fed to their livestock grain which they might instead have sold for a high price. A third group, principally the farmers of North and South Dakota and certain sections of Minnesota and Montana, failed because of their one-crop systems and their frequent short crops. Many of these farmers had taken up wheat raising under the stimulus of high wartime prices. The land upon which they farmed was often marginal and would have required the talents of the most efficient farmers to produce good crops. Montana's heavy proportion of failure was, in part, a reflection of misfits attempting to farm nonagricultural and marginal lands. In the areas of heaviest failure in that state, 51 per cent of those who went on the land

42. Seligman, *Economics of Farm Relief*, pp. 20–22; Nourse, *Government in Relation to Agriculture*, p. 881; Baker, in *Annals of the American Academy*, CXLI (March, 1929), p. 117.

43. David Friday, "The Course of Agricultural Income during the Last Twenty-Five Years," *American Economic Review, Supplement*, XIII (March, 1923), pp. 156–57.

were without previous farming experience, and 30 per cent had no capital.[44] Among them were men from sixty-three occupations other than farming. "There were two circus musicians, a paper hanger, a sailor, a sea-going engineer, two wrestlers, two barbers, a cigar maker, a race horse man, a bricklayer, an undertaker, a deep-sea diver, six old maids, a milliner, and a professional gambler." The fact that such people exposed themselves to the hazards of a single crop increased the risk they took. A fourth group of farmers failed because of their inefficiency. Their production costs were simply too high.[45]

For a while the postwar depression in agriculture was paralleled by a similar depression in industry, business, and finance. After the spring of 1920 industrial production fell off rapidly and price levels began to sag. By the end of the year, wage cuts were common and unemployment had become a serious problem. The year 1921 was dark for industry and agriculture alike, but for most business activities other than farming the depression was fading out by the end of 1922 and recovery was beginning. Thereafter, from 1923 to 1929, the nation's business, except for agriculture and a few industries, experienced a long period of steady expansion, marred only by a few minor setbacks. Iron, steel, and coal production mounted steadily, trade revived, and a veritable boom developed. The seemingly insatiable demand of the American public for automobiles, radios, electric washing machines, electric refrigerators, and the like, accompanied by a widespread use of installment buying and supported by an equally insistent demand for housing, made for a general appearance of prosperity, at least for most of the nonfarm population. Much of this prosperity eventually turned out to be more illusory than real, for the position of organized labor was weak and unemployment was slowly but surely growing in some industries. But the bulk of the nonfarm population and its leaders believed that a permanent plateau of prosperity had been reached, and the farmers were envious.[46] Speaking in Paris in the

44. John H. Rich, *The Economic Position of Agriculture in the Northwestern Grain Areas* (Minneapolis, 1922), p. 7.
45. Friday, in *American Economic Review, Supplement*, XIII (March, 1923), p. 156–57.
46. Reginald C. McGrane, *The Economic Development of the American Nation* (Boston, 1942), pp. 547–49; George Soule, *Prosperity Decade, From War to Depression, 1917–1929* (New York, 1947), pp. 107–26, 208–28, 275–84.

fall of 1918, Senator James Hamilton Lewis of Illinois had declared, "We are going to hear from the farmers as never before. They will tell us that their profits have been limited and their businesses regulated during the war, while others have been getting rich because of the war, without restraint. This protest of the farmer will be a big factor two years hence."[47] The senator was right, but if he could have foreseen that the farmer was soon to find himself in a state of depression with most of the city population in a state of prosperity, he would have expanded his rhetoric. The country would indeed hear from the farmer.

47. *Wallaces' Farmer*, XLIII (September 20, 1918), p. 1329.

Chapter V

THE AMERICAN SOCIETY OF EQUITY

THE EXCESSIVE individualism of the American farmer has long been a subject of extensive historical comment. Frederick Jackson Turner lost no opportunity to emphasize this characteristic in his studies of the American frontier. American individualism, Turner believed, was itself largely a frontier product, since in every frontier region each pioneer farmer had to work out his own salvation with a minimum of assistance from his fellow men. The decline of subsistence farming and the rise of production for sale made extensive alterations in the farmer's way of life, for under the new conditions he was as much a businessman as a producer. Contacts with the outside world for such necessities as credit, transportation, marketing, and merchandising were unavoidable. And yet each farmer preferred to stand aloof from every other farmer as much as he dared. In a sense, as has often been noted, each farm, even in thickly settled areas, was in itself a little frontier, and each farm boundary a kind of frontier line. Farmers were obliged most of the time to work alone or in family units, not shoulder to shoulder with other workers after the fashion of factory operatives. Their contacts with other farmers, at least from the point of view of the city dweller, were few and far between. They looked with the suspicion of rivals at what went on across their fences in their neighbors' fields. Every farmer thought of himself, in a sense, as a competitor with every other farmer; and such, indeed, he tended to be.

Thus the task of organizing the farmers in their own defense was formidable in the extreme. As small producers, each standing alone, they were deplorably weak in bargaining power, but they clung tenaciously to their independence and resisted with all their might those same possibilities for united action that so intrigued the men with whom they had to deal. Their business adversaries, perhaps because they were fewer in numbers, less isolated, and on the whole better educated, got together. City laborers joined forces in powerful unions to fight for what they believed to be their rights. But the discontented farmers, faced by similar circumstances, were reluctant to organize. Often they preferred flight to the nearest frontier, as long as the frontier remained, or even flight to the city in search of a job. Only when times grew excessively hard were they willing to surrender a small portion of their independence to achieve something resembling a united front.[1]

During the late nineteenth century two such periods of stress and strain —one in the seventies and the other in the late eighties and the early nineties—actually drove the farmers together, at least in certain portions of the Middle West and the South. The first period of distress produced the Granger movement; the second, the Farmers' Alliance and Populism. But as soon as agriculture prospered again, these organizations fell apart. By the early twentieth century the Grange had reverted to the status of a cultural and educational body, as its founders had originally intended it to be; furthermore, it had shifted the center of its activities to the northeast, and was strongest in New England and the Middle Atlantic states. As for the Farmers' Alliance, it had evaporated into thin air, while Populism, whatever ideas of political reform it might have contributed to the older parties, had lost its status as an independent movement.

The economic disorders of the 1920's were sufficiently acute to bring into prominence another group of agricultural organizations. Most of these orders, however, dated well back into the prewar years, and some of them had already had short periods of vigorous activity. The prosperity of the early twentieth century was by no means equally distributed, and

1. On this general subject see W. S. Harwood, "Coöperation in the West," *Atlantic Monthly*, LXXXV (April, 1900), p. 540; J. R. Elliot, *American Farms* (New York, 1890), p. 125; C. Vincent, "Cooperation Among Western Farmers," *Arena*, XXXI (March, 1904), p. 287.

2. K. L. Butterfield, "The Grange," *The Forum*, XXXI (April, 1901), p. 233.

areas of considerable discontent could be found at any time. Moreover, for farmers who faced the fact that such prosperity as they enjoyed stemmed far too much from rising land values and far too little from the sale of produce, there were also ample grounds for worry at any time. Some farmers were learning, too, as the cooperative movement abundantly attests, that they could accomplish much more when many stood together than when each man stood alone.[3]

One of the earliest of the twentieth century farm orders to achieve some degree of prominence was the American Society of Equity, which was founded in Indianapolis on December 24, 1902. The man who claimed full credit for the founding of Equity, and for the plan of action by which the order hoped to better the lot of the farmer, was James A. Everitt, publisher of an Indianapolis journal known as *Up-to-Date Farming and Gardening*. Everitt also owned a feed and seed business by means of which he augmented his income from printing and publishing and increased his contacts with the farmers. He claimed, however, to spend much time in thought; indeed, his every waking moment, he said, was given over to "originating ideas and revolving plans in my brain." In time an anti-Everitt faction arose in Equity which asserted that Everitt was no more the founder of the order than he was the author of the Bible. This faction pinned its faith to W. L. Hearron of Carlinville, Illinois, from whom it claimed Everitt had filched all his best ideas, but the fact remains that Everitt's newspaper, together with a highly emotional volume entitled *The Third Power*, which he published in 1903, were principally responsible for launching the organization.[4]

Everitt thought of himself as a strictly practical man, and, as he saw it, the object of his order was primarily to contribute to the farmers' profits.

3. Gerald Goldstein, "The Economic Basis of Agrarian Unrest in the Progressive Period" (unpublished master's thesis, University of California, 1948).

4. James A. Everitt, *The Third Power* (Indianapolis, 1903), pp. 246–47; R. H. Bahmer, "The American Society of Equity," *Agricultural History*, XIV (January, 1940), pp. 33–35; J. L. Nash, "Building a Farmers' Monopoly," *World Today*, XIII (July, 1907), p. 717; *Wisconsin Equity News* (Madison), June 1, 1908, p. 13; *ibid.*, June 10, 1912, pp. 1–2; Robert Lee Hunt, *A History of Farmer Movements in the Southwest, 1873–1925* (College Station, Texas, 1935), pp. 104–8; American Society of Equity, *The Plan of the American Society of Equity* (Indianapolis, n.d.), p. 1 [pamphlet].

What he had in mind was essentially a gigantic holding movement. Why shouldn't the farmers set prices themselves instead of allowing "the captains of industry, the promoter, the underwriter, the labor leader, and the grain gambler" to dictate to them? By devising some simple machinery for setting prices, and by keeping farm produce off the market unless and until these prices could be obtained, Everitt was certain that the farmers could not only secure relief from the ill effects of monopoly; they could themselves, in fact, become the greatest of all monopolists.[5]

Everitt was much concerned with the necessity of holding down the "visible supply" of any given commodity, for it was this "visible supply" which in relation to the demand tended at any given time to fix the price. He believed that wherever possible the farmers should provide storage facilities for their own crops on their own farms. If forced to it, however, they could "put up granaries, elevators or warehouses to hold their products, or build cooperative cold storage plants to hold their fruit, etc." But he was chary of the business complications that resulted from joint-stock companies, or even cooperatives after the Granger pattern. The farmers should keep out of all business except the farming business as completely as possible. All they need try to do was to put farming itself "on a safe profitable basis," with benefits for the farmer "equaling those realized in other business undertakings."[6]

The violent fluctuations in prices from which the farmers continually lost while the speculators gained, Everitt believed to be entirely unnecessary. The farmers could change all this if only they would stop dumping the bulk of any particular commodity on the market at harvest time. What they needed was some method of feeding the market with a twelve-month supply on a twelve-month basis. Everitt was sure that this could be done if only a fraction of the producers—the more intelligent ones—would join forces. He had no notion that all the nation's wheat growers, for example, could be persuaded to hold their wheat off the market. But if the organized farmers could control no more than half the total amount of wheat normally exported, he insisted, they would be in a position to se

5. Everitt, *The Third Power*, third edition (1905), p. 35; fourth edition (1907) p. vii.
6. *Plan of the American Society of Equity*, pp. 2–3; Bahmer, in *Agricultural History*, XIV (January, 1940), p. 37.

a just and equitable price. As he saw it, a million farmers working together through a single agency could control the surplus and assure the producers the fair prices they ought to have. Some of Everitt's ideas even foreshadowed McNary-Haugenism. He believed that the farmers, by standing firm in their demand for a high selling price, could take full advantage of tariff protection. "What is the use of having a tariff," he asked, "if it don't benefit the wheat growers? Farmers get together and make this tariff effective."[7]

In his obsession with price control as the one sure remedy for the farmers' ills, Everitt tended to close his eyes to the related problem of how to limit production. In his earlier statements he clearly had both problems in mind. "If it was possible," he wrote in 1901, "to control and limit the production of our chief farm crops, within the action of the farmers themselves, it would be possible to control prices." But eventually he reasoned himself into the belief that there would be no need to worry about surplus production. The American people were consuming more food all the time, and they would need still more in the future. Soon they would be able to consume all the foodstuffs the farmers could possibly produce. All that was really needed was careful and systematic marketing of the available supply. Some of his statements indicate that Everitt envisaged something closely akin to Henry A. Wallace's "ever normal granary":

Every person has noted that a season of scarcity usually follows a season of plenty, or in case of a bountiful crop one year the next is likely to be much shorter. With profitable prices fixed for each farm crop, it will soon be very easy for farmers to hold their grain over to make up for shortages that are bound to exist. Thus the seasons of plenty will help out seasons of scarcity.[8]

Had Everitt lived a few decades later, it is possible that his services as an agricultural expert might have been in great demand. He would certainly have found much that was familiar to him in the parity concept. Beginning with the premise that "farmers are under neither legal nor moral obligation to feed the balance of the world at an unprofitably low

7. *Plan of the American Society of Equity*, p. 3; Everitt, *The Third Power*, third edition, pp. 284, 291; fourth edition, p. 275; Bahmer, in *Agricultural History*, XIV (January, 1940), p. 37.
8. Quoted, *ibid.*, pp. 35–37.

price," Everitt argued that it should be possible to "remove agriculture from the list of uncertain industries and place it on a basis of certainty for prices equal to that enjoyed by the best regulated manufacturing or commercial enterprises." Farming had become a business and it was high time that farmers behaved as businessmen. Other businesses had discarded competition in their quest for profits and had sought to "control the market." They entered without scruple into combinations "to limit output, to lift prices, to regulate wages, and to 'work' the government." It was up to the farmers to adopt similar methods; they were just as much entitled to fix prices as the manufacturers were—more so, indeed, since agriculture was the most important segment in our economy. "We might survive the loss of our steel mills, but if our farms were to quit producing the country would go to ruin. Why should not the farmers be supreme? And if they strive for something less than supremacy—namely mere parity with the rest of our people—ought they not to be encouraged?"[9]

The structure and control of Equity was highly centralized, at least from its beginning until the house cleaning of 1907. The official publication, *Up-To-Date Farming*, remained in the private control and ownership of Everitt; in fact, a subscription to the "official paper" was considered adequate to bring one the full benefits of membership. For all practical purposes, the national union consisted of a seven-man board of directors, which was supposed to be in constant session. One did not have to belong to a local union, but locals of ten or more members might be organized by persons of "good moral character" who paid a membership fee of $1.50 and annual dues of $1.00. Those under twenty-one or over seventy-five and the wives of farmers were admitted free and paid no dues.[10]

Everitt and his paper, aided by the national board of directors, were supposed to shape the marketing policies of the society and to serve as a clearinghouse for agricultural information. A crop-reporting service was an integral part of the marketing program. The secretaries of locals were required to obtain annual reports on their crops from all members, although the precise nature of these reports was not specific. On the basis

9. *Plan of the American Society of Equity*, p. 1; Everitt, *The Third Power*, third edition, pp. 6, 9, 23–24, 71; fourth edition, p. vii.

10. Bahmer, in *Agricultural History*, XIV (January, 1940), pp. 38, 40; *Plan of the American Society of Equity*, p. 1.

of information so obtained, the board of directors, each of whom was supposed to be an expert in some line of agriculture, was to study the demands of the nation and then place what it considered to be an equitable price on each commodity. Ideally, there should also be held annually "a convention of wheat growers, of corn raisers, of cotton planters, of tobacco raisers, of fruit growers, of livestock men—of every great agricultural interest" to consider the supply, demand, market, and price and all other questions that affected the industry. Such "equitable prices" as were set by the board of directors were also referred to as "minimum prices," below which the farmers were urged not to sell. "There need be no fear," wrote Everitt, "that buyers will be out of the market long, because the world must have your goods all the time."[11]

The name Equity had something appealing about it. It was synonymous with justice, equality, parity, fairness, righteousness, and honesty. The order was also referred to as the "American Square Deal Association," no doubt after the "Square Deal" of Theodore Roosevelt.

An analysis of the backgrounds of twelve men prominent in early Equity councils reveals precisely what one would expect. All claimed to have had farming experience of one kind or another, vocational or avocational. Three had had teaching experience and one had been a member of Congress. At least five claimed to have attended or to have graduated from college. Two had had newspaper experience and one had been a customs collector under two different presidents. A number had been members of the Farmers' Alliance and the Populist party. One who was to assume an important role was an osteopath who had "an active interest in religion and politics, [and] sociology, believing heartily in the philosophy of Jesus Christ, the Fatherhood of God and the Brotherhood of Man; [and] that we are our brother's keeper."[12]

As might be expected with such leadership, the membership and organizing policies of the Equity Society were highly defective. Apparently Everitt had had little experience as an organizer before his founding of the order. The membership dues of one dollar, really the subscription price of his paper, was far too small a sum to cover the costs of organizing; yet

11. *Ibid.*, pp. 1–2; Everitt, *The Third Power,* third edition, pp. 231–32, 273–77.
12. *Ibid.,* fourth edition, pp. 214–15; *Wisconsin Equity News,* February 10, 1912, . 1; *Equity Farm Journal* (Indianapolis), I (November, 1908), p. 6.

Everitt expected to recruit a million members, and with their support to usher in an era of profitable prices by the control of marketing. But even at this nominal fee the farmers were slow to respond. Equity obtained only about twenty or thirty thousand members during its first few months of existence, which was far short of the several hundred thousand which Everitt had anticipated. Hoping to speed up the drive for membership, Everitt lowered the rates, first to fifty cents and then to twenty-five, but all to no avail. He had hoped, too, also in vain, that these reductions would curb rumors that he was building up his fortune at the expense of the society.[13]

What membership figures are available are incomplete and perhaps unreliable. In 1906, one estimate placed the number at 200,000, but it appears unlikely that the society had more than 100,000 members at its peak. In 1907, the number was placed at 60,000, and in October, 1908, at 26,259. By the latter year state organizations, which were no part of the original scheme, had been formed in Arkansas, Illinois, Indiana, Kansas, Kentucky, Michigan, Minnesota, Nebraska, New York, North Dakota, Oklahoma, South Dakota, Virginia, and Wisconsin, but Equity attained its greatest strength in Kentucky, Wisconsin, Minnesota, the Dakotas, and Montana.[14]

During the early years the price-setting activities of Equity revolved chiefly around wheat and tobacco. Wheat appears to have had primary place on the agenda. In 1903 Everitt distributed the first of a series of "Dollar Wheat Bulletins" urging the farmers to hold their wheat for a dollar a bushel. The following year he asked them to demand $1.20 a bushel. At the same time he also appealed to the southern farmers to hold their cotton, but the cotton growers apparently preferred to join organizations with a southern background, such as the Southern Cotton Association or the Farmers' Union, and paid little attention to Equity. In 1904 an organization of tobacco producers was established in Lynchburg, Virginia, largely under the influence of Equity, and late that same year the society began to attract attention in the tobacco fields of Kentucky and

13. Everitt, *The Third Power,* third edition, pp. 280, 284; *Wisconsin Equity News*, June 10, 1912, p. 2.

14. *Indian-Arbiter* (Ada, Okla.), March 1, 1906, p. 12; *Equity Farm Journal,* (November, 1907), p. 2; (October, 1908), p. 9; (January, 1908), p. 9.

Tennessee. By 1907, some headway was reported, also, among the spring wheat producers of the agricultural Northwest and the tobacco fields of Wisconsin.[15]

Meanwhile some sentiment had developed in favor of "direct trade between the producers and consumers" so that "organized farmers and organized laborers" could cooperate more effectively. In the hope of fulfilling this ambition, nine farmers representing Equity appeared on November 14, 1906, before the national convention of the American Federation of Labor in Minneapolis. Plans were discussed "to effect an honest, quick and practical means of exchange of the products of the farm and also the products of organized labor as identified by the 'Union Label.' " The ultimate result of this meeting was the short-lived International Equity Exchange.[16]

The leader in this movement was M. Wes Tubbs, national secretary of Equity, who had grown increasingly skeptical of Everitt's crop-holding, price-fixing program and believed that more could be accomplished by orthodox methods of cooperative marketing. Through Tubbs' efforts, three joint-stock cooperatives were organized in Chicago, Detroit, and Scranton, Pennsylvania. In each city the local federation of labor supported the idea on the theory that union members would be able to save money by dealing directly with the producers through an exchange. Tubbs finally got a charter in New Jersey for the International Equity Exchange, which was designed to act as a holding company for local exchanges. Tubbs hoped eventually to develop an extensive system of country shipping exchanges for the use of the farmers, as well as city exchanges for the storage and shipment of farm produce. Perhaps his scheme was no less chimerical than Everitt's, at least in the extent to which he believed it could be made effective.[17]

Naturally this development was viewed by Everitt with the greatest misgivings, for the founder of the order had committed himself to the

15. Everitt, *The Third Power*, third edition, pp. 220–23; fourth edition, pp. 226–); *Western Tobacco Journal* (Cincinnati), XXXI (November 14, 1904), p. 1; XXII (January 16, 1905), p. 2; (March 13, 1905), p. 1; (November 27, 1905), p. (October 23, 1905), pp. 1–2.

16. *Equity Farm Journal*, I (May, 1908), p. 5; International Equity Exchange, *The Farmers' New Marketing System* (Madison, Wis., 1908), pp. 16–22 [pamphlet].

17. Bahmer, in *Agricultural History*, XIV (January, 1940), pp. 53–54.

principle that the total energies of Equity should go toward price fixing, and he was now particularly absorbed in trying to fix the price of wheat. Everitt had considerable evidence to show that his propaganda had been making good progress in the wheat-growing areas, especially in North Dakota, where a state organization had been set up and a grain growers' branch was contemplated. Under these circumstances, he deplored the distraction that Tubbs' activities provided. Furthermore, he had been opposed all along to joint-stock business cooperatives of the type that Tubbs had organized. The way was thus wide-open for a violent split in Equity, and at the national convention of 1907 the split came.[18]

There was more to the opposition to Everitt than a mere difference of opinion on principle. Tubbs and others were concerned over the way in which Everitt sought to dominate the society; some had even suggested that the order should be rechristened "The American Society of Everitt." And there were other charges, even more disturbing. Everitt was accused of mishandling the funds of the national organization. He had apparently made no effort to separate the accounts of the seed store, the printing establishment, and Equity, which were all in his building. Auditors who examined the organization records, which were handled by Everitt's own bookkeeper, found them "all mixed up, the seed business, the printing plant and the society's own accounts, and it was simply impossible . . to straighten [them] out." Many felt that at the very least, Everitt had been conducting his business in a manner unbecoming the head of a farmers' organization.[19]

A subject of particularly bitter contention was the fifty-year contract which Everitt had negotiated with the society for publishing its official paper. Irritation over this situation came to a head because of mounting complaints that Everitt had refused to publish material that certain members had submitted to him. A group of investigators later reported that the contract was not binding because Everitt, an executive of Equity and the party of the first part, could not "sign a contract or make a contract" with himself as an individual, the party of the second part. In other words Everitt could not legally enter into a contract with himself. When mem-

18. *Ibid.*, pp. 54–55.
19. *Annual Meeting of the North Dakota State Union of the American Society of Equity* (Devils Lake, N. Dak., November 19, 1907), pp. 28–30.

bers of the society asked him what he would take for his paper, he priced it at $75,000, an exaggerated price which naturally was rejected.[20]

Whatever the truth of the matter may have been, the convention of 1907 deposed Everitt and elected a new slate of officers headed by C. M. Barnett of Kentucky as president. Completely unreconciled to the change, Everitt organized a short-lived rival order, the Farmers' Society of Equity, as a spite move, obviously designed to drain the original Equity of its membership. Bitter warfare, with violent charges and countercharges, followed, to the detriment of both the orders. Many farmers continued to subscribe to *Up-To-Date Farming,* thinking that they were paying dues to the American Society of Equity, while others, who had grown disgusted with the turn of events, refused to have any further dealings with either body.[21]

The departure of Everitt from the presidency marked a sharp break in the policies of the Equity. Plans for controlling production were gradually relaxed and greater stress was placed on cooperative marketing and buying. Also, the organization became highly decentralized, as opposed to the earlier practice of centering authority in Indianapolis. The result was an unwieldly collection of state and commodity organizations, theoretically but not practically bound to the parent body, with a common name and common enemies, but influenced in their various activities more by local interests than by a general agricultural program. In fact, the American Society of Equity, as a national organization, had suffered mortal wounds from which it never fully recovered.

An early manifestation of the new spirit of autonomy in Equity occurred during the wars waged by the tobacco producers of Kentucky and Tennessee against the tobacco trust. This episode, in which Equity played a leading role, marked the last, as well as the most conspicuous, effort of the society to put its production-control and price-fixing policies into operation. It was also a classic illustration of the possibilities open when a group of agriculturists band together in an effort to exact fair prices from a giant corporation.

By 1900 the American Tobacco Company, or the "tobacco trust," as it

20. *Ibid.,* pp. 35–36.
21. *You Have Been Deceived and Betrayed By Your Trusted Representatives* Indianapolis, 1907), p. 28 [pamphlet]; *Equity Farm Journal,* I (October, 1908), . 7; III (February 1, 1910), p. 12.

was more commonly called, had reduced the growers of tobacco to a hope-lessly unsatisfactory bargaining position. This condition was no doubt promoted considerably by the infiltration into the tobacco areas of an army of illiterate tenant farmers who raised tobacco on share leases with no other hope of betterment than what they might obtain by an increase in their acreage.[22] This situation exactly suited the trust, which was not satisfied with its control of the manufacturing and marketing processes, but expected also to dictate the prices paid for tobacco to the original producers. The resulting low prices, coupled with high living and pro-duction costs, created among the tobacco growers a situation of acute poverty and distress.[23]

Some of the tobacco producers had felt the need of organizing well before Equity appeared on the scene and had discussed plans for the or-ganization of a "farmers' tobacco trust" as early as 1901. Agitation for controlling production became more common during 1903 and 1904. By 1904 agitators were urging the farmers to "grow no more tobacco," or to "cut down the crop to half," or to "grow only 25 per cent of a crop." Equity appears to have received serious mention for the first time in 1904, and Equity members seem to have taken an important part in the holding movement of 1905 that resulted in substantially higher prices. But such groups as the Dark Tobacco Growers' Protective Association, the Burley Growers' Association of Kentucky, and no doubt others—all with similar ideas—had either preceded Equity or were contemporaries of it.[24]

The object of Equity, when it appeared on the scene, was to consolidate

22. Report of the Commissioner of Corporation on the Tobacco Industry, Part I, Position of the Tobacco Combination in the Industry (3 parts, Washington, 1909-15), pp. 14-15; John L. Mathews, "Agrarian Pooling in Kentucky," Charities and the Commons, XX (1908), p. 193.

23. Hearings on the Bills for the Relief of Tobacco Growers (59 Congress, 2 ses-sion, Senate Document 372, Vol. VI, Washington, 1907), p. 42; Anna Youngman, "The Tobacco Pools of Kentucky and Tennessee," Journal of Political Economy, XVIII (January, 1910), p. 36; H. C. Filley, Cooperation in Agriculture (New York, 1929), pp. 246-471.

24. Western Tobacco Journal, XXVIII (January 14, 1901), p. 1; XXX (Jan-uary 5, 1903), p. 1; (February 2, 1903), p. 2; (February 9, 1903), p. 2; (April 2, 1903), p. 2; (May 11, 1903), p. 4; (May 18, 1903), p. 1; XXXI (January 14, 1904), p. 4; (February 29, 1904), p. 2; (August 22, 1904), p. 2; XXX (April 22, 1903), p. 2.

or absorb all these local groups. In 1906 it took the lead in a "forty-day whirlwind campaign" to obtain pledges from the farmers not to dispose of their crop at the prices offered by the trust. This campaign succeeded so well that on January 2, 1907, according to one report, about 58 per cent of an estimated 92,000 acres planted to tobacco for the year was pledged to the newly organized Burley Tobacco Society.[25]

Even more aggressive action was planned for the 1907 crop. Equity officials sought to "produce a short crop and sell it for a long price." They also suggested that tobacco factories be established in the event that the American Tobacco Company failed to purchase the 1906 and 1907 crops. On July 11, with some 103,000 acres out of an estimated 135,000 planted reportedly in the pool, representatives of the tobacco associations from Wisconsin, North Carolina, South Carolina, Pennsylvania, and other states planned a meeting with representatives from Ohio, Indiana, and Kentucky to organize a tobacco association covering the entire country. In the fall of 1907, the Burley Society formally announced that it would attempt to eliminate the 1908 crop altogether.[26]

Despite the various methods employed to facilitate organization, difficulties of the most trying character arose. The unfavorable system of land-tenure system, the indifference of the slow, lethargic, and incompetent farmer, the financial disabilities of most producers, and the financial strength of trust opposition impeded action. Fortunately, both the Planters' Protective Association and the Burley Society received considerable assistance from their few well-to-do members, as well as from equally sympathetic warehousemen in Louisville and Cincinnati who saw their business menaced.[27]

Perhaps more irritating than even the expected trust opposition was the attitude of the independent farmer who refused to join the association,

25. *Wisconsin Equity News*, June 1, 1908, p. 4; *Western Tobacco Journal*, XXXIV (January 7, 1907), p. 1; Everitt, *The Third Power*, fourth edition, p. 289.
26. *Western Tobacco Journal*, XXXIV (March 18, 1907), p. 1; (May 13, 1907), p. 7; (July 15, 1907), p. 1; (November 4, 1907), p. 1.
27. Youngman, in *Journal of Political Economy*, XVIII (January, 1910), pp. 40–41; John L. Mathews, "The Farmers' Union and the Tobacco Pool," *Atlantic Monthly*, CII (October, 1908), p. 484; *Wisconsin Equity News*, June 1, 1908, p. 5; R. Bache, "The Great Tobacco Strike," *Technical World*, VI (1907), p. 604; Youngman, in *Journal of Political Economy*, XVIII (January, 1910), p. 43.

either because he was convinced that it offered no hopes for betterment, or because he suspected the organizers, or because he was already enjoying the benefit of higher prices. Pooling members deeply resented the tendency of the occasional independent, or "hillbilly," as he might be called contemptuously, to cash in on the higher prices the holding movement had achieved. Why should one producer join the organization, pay fees, and endure hardships while another who refused to cooperate sold at a fancy profit?[28]

Aroused by this situation, some of the tobacco growers finally decided to employ force in order to achieve conformity. Their "night riders" used the whip or even the rifle on independents or farmers who "talked too much"; they brutally assaulted tobacco buyers, they set fires, sowed plant beds with salt or grass seed, and even dynamited machinery. One terror-stricken farmer found a grave dug in the midst of one of his plant beds.[29]

The effects of these acts of violence on the tobacco country were devastating. As selling tobacco independently of the farmers' association became dangerous, neighbors became suspicious of one another and terror prevailed everywhere. Courts of law were paralyzed by perjury, packed juries, or fear on the part of witnesses to testify against known marauders. Hundreds of farmers left the tobacco areas in search of homes elsewhere. So widespread was the disorder that in 1907, the secretary of the Kentucky Board of Fire Underwriters cautioned residents of the affected areas that "unless confidence can be restored, the companies will refuse indemnity to all handlers of tobacco."[30]

While innumerable obstacles had threatened to defeat the elimination program in 1908, in actual fact the acreage devoted to tobacco was held at a low minimum. In the Burley country the estimated acreage fell to 18 per cent of normal, and in the dark-tobacco country also sharp reductions

28. *Wisconsin Equity News,* June 1, 1908, p. 6; Mathews, in *Atlantic Monthly,* CII (October, 1908), pp. 489–90.

29. Youngman, in *Journal of Political Economy,* XVIII (January, 1910), p. 45 C. M. Meacham, *A History of Christian County, Kentucky* (Nashville, 1930), pp 346–48; J. C. Miller, *The Black Patch War* (Chapel Hill, N. C., 1936), pp. 16–17

30. E. A. Jonas, "The Night-Riders: A Trust of Farmers," *World's Work,* XVII (February, 1909), p. 11217; Marie Taylor, "Night Riders in the Black Patch" (unpublished master's thesis, University of Kentucky, 1934), p. 38.

were effected. Western market receipts which in 1889 were placed at 300,000 hogsheads had dwindled to about 110,000 in 1909.[31]

After long-drawn-out negotiations, on November 19, 1908, the American Tobacco Company and the Burley Tobacco Society finally consummated what was considered the largest tobacco transaction in history. Between 60 and 70 million pounds of Burley changed hands for a cash consideration of between 12 and 13 million dollars. According to the agreement, the company was to buy 75 per cent of the 80 million pounds in the 1907 pool at an average price of 17 cents a pound, totaling about $10,000,000, and 75 per cent of the estimated 13 to 15 million pounds of the 1906 crop at an average of between 20 and 21 cents a pound, bringing an additional $2,000,000. This left the pool still in possession of 25 per cent of the Burley crop, which became an exciting subject of discussion. Some believed that it was being held for the independent manufacturers who had been the allies of the Burley and Equity societies; others maintained that the American Tobacco Company had wanted the remaining 25 per cent to squeeze the independents out of business.[32]

Once the tobacco deal had been completed, accounts of the anxious moments experienced by both sides during the pooling period began to be told. The Burley Society, so the story ran, had to contend on the one hand with the American Tobacco Company and its untold millions of dollars, while on the other hand it faced impending demoralization in Equity ranks. Had the war lasted sixty days longer, the pool would probably have disintegrated. The tobacco company also had its problems. Its reserve stocks had dwindled; the 1908 crop was small and the big demand from independent manufacturers had caused alarm for the company's future supplies. Then, too, the activity of Thomas J. Ryan, the dominant spirit of the company, had been an important factor. He wanted peace and harmony restored because of the "effect and influence such action might have with the government in its prosecution of the Tobacco Trust as an illegal combination in restraint of trade."[33]

31. *Ibid.*, p. 23; E. H. Mathewson, *The Export and Manufacturing Tobaccos of the United States*, U. S. Dept. Agri., Bureau of Plant Industry, Bulletin 244 (Washington, 1912), pp. 47–48, 250–51; Filley, *Cooperation in Agriculture*, pp. 25–51.

32. *Cincinnati Enquirer*, November 20, 26, 1908.

33. *Ibid.*, November 21, 1908.

By 1909 the Equity movement was on the decline in Kentucky and Tennessee. Dissatisfaction had developed over the prices which the farmers received; the possible benefits of production control were disputed by many growers who had taken part in the farm strike of 1908; and the administrative policies of Equity and its subsidiary organization had become matters of heated controversy. Some believed that with the price rise of 1908, the marketing troubles of the tobacco growers were at an end, but tobacco production took an upward swing in 1909, as usual after a good price year, and with it, the marketing problem reappeared. For many Equity left bitter memories, and they wanted no more of it. Still, the farmers had something to show for their troubles. They had cooperated in building a number of warehouses; they had obtained better grading methods and a tobacco factory; and they had demonstrated the potentialities of organized action.[34]

Meanwhile, Equity was slowly but surely rooting itself in Wisconsin and the spring wheat regions of the agricultural Northwest. It was here that the society gained its greatest strength; in fact, such local organizations as the Wisconsin Society of Equity and the autonomous Equity Cooperative Exchange dwarfed the national organization into insignificance. Equity began its activities in Wisconsin in 1903, expanded rapidly, and by 1920 could claim a paid-up membership of 40,000. At first, the Wisconsin Equity sought higher prices for farm products by a voluntary curtailment of the output, but later it encouraged the growth of cooperative marketing and purchasing associations and sought legislation favorable to these ends.[35]

As in Kentucky and Tennessee, the Wisconsin Equity was influenced by various local developments, both economic and political. It attracted its first substantial support in the wheat-growing river counties of the

34. *Western Tobacco Journal*, XXXVI (June 28, 1909), p. 7; (July 19, 1909), pp. 1–2; (July 26, 1909), pp. 1–2; (August 2, 1909), p. 4; (July 19, 1909), pp. 1–2. Also B. H. Hibbard, *Marketing Agricultural Products* (New York, 1921), p. 238; Filley, *Cooperation in Agriculture*, pp. 251–52; Youngman, in *Journal of Political Economy*, XVIII (January, 1910), p. 42.

35. Everitt, *The Third Power*, fourth edition, pp. 269–70; J. G. Thomson, *The Rise and Decline of the Wheat Growing Industry in Wisconsin* (Madison, Wis. 1909), pp. 82, 99.

upper Mississippi Valley, where agricultural discontent was an old story.[36] Here the Scandinavian element was strong, and blood ties tended to supplement the economic unity which stemmed from the common problems experienced by grain growers. Many farmers in this area had strong reminiscences of the Granger and Populist campaigns, particularly those waged by the great Minnesota orator, Ignatius Donnelly. Their minds were thus well prepared for the propaganda put out by Equity organizers and La Follette supporters alike. Both groups were antimonopolistic in philosophy. To La Follette and his followers, monopoly and graft were the principal corrupting influences in government; to the Equity leaders, these same forces—in the form of middlemen, boards of trade, bankers, and railroad interests—were responsible for the depressed agricultural prices. Both were fighting on a common ground but were utilizing different methods of attack.[37]

Another contribution to the growth of the organization came from the Wisconsin tobacco farmers, who suffered no less than the farmers of Kentucky and Tennessee from an "antiquated" and "unscientific" system of marketing. Because of its interest in these difficulties, Equity had penetrated into the tobacco areas of the state to such an extent that, according to the *Milwaukee Journal*, it had won complete control of the tobacco production in the important Edgerton area by 1907 and could threaten to eliminate the entire crop the following year. Within a year the tobacco farmers had built or leased a substantial number of tobacco warehouses in the southern and southwestern part of the state, but their attempt to duplicate the feat of the tobacco farmers of Kentucky and Tennessee by eliminating the crop and "letting the demand catch up with the supply" ended in failure.[38]

36. *Equity News* (Madison, Wis.), December 1, 1915, p. 234.
37. Robert M. La Follette, *La Follette's Autobiography: A Personal Narrative of Political Experience* (Madison, Wis., 1913), pp. 18–19; A. P. Wilder, "Governor La Follette and What He Stands For," *Outlook*, LXX (March 8, 1902), p. 631; Henrietta M. Larson, *The Wheat Market and the Farmer in Minnesota, 1858–1900* (New York, 1926), pp. 249–50; André Siegfried, *America Comes of Age* (New York, 1927), pp. 287–88.
38. "Cooperative Tobacco Marketing in Wisconsin," Wisconsin State Department of Markets, *Bulletin*, Vol. IV, No. 4, pp. 8–9; *Milwaukee Journal*, October 26, 1907; *Wisconsin Equity News*, May 1, 1908, p. 6.

Once the Wisconsin Society of Equity was under way, it began to level a barrage of criticism against the state agricultural college. The school was as obnoxious from the farmer's point of view, Equity critics said, as the middlemen, the grain gamblers, and the corporations. As far as the average farmer was concerned, the university was a "cold-storage institution of dead languages and useless learning which costs several millions of bushels of wheat each year." Furthermore, the college of agriculture was too "productive-minded." Its traditional policy was to encourage the farmers to increase production on the theory that agriculture, like industry, had to be made as efficient as possible. Equity leaders insisted that this attitude on the part of the college not only failed to better the farmers' position, but actually hurt them because of the heavy surpluses which it promoted. According to one Equity spokesman, who insisted that the society had no desire to "cross swords" with the college, there was pertinence in the thought that peach growers were interested not so much in Bordeaux mixture, while peaches were rotting, as they were in selling their products at profitable prices.[39]

Equity critics also charged that the college offered courses which were not only far removed from the economic needs of future farmers but actually made students lose their taste for rural life. Thus as a result of their college experience, farm youths drifted to the city instead of returning to the farm. The same critics held that professors of agriculture lacked practical farm experience and were unsympathetic with farm difficulties. The college of agriculture remained aloof from farm organizations and did nothing to help solve the farmers' marketing problems. Indeed, why should one not assume that it was actually doing the bidding of the corporations?

The *Wisconsin Equity News* made innumerable demands for a legislative investigation of university courses and university expenditures. When it was announced in 1909 that the university baseball team was planning a trip to the Orient, this journal remarked protestingly: "It is time for the investigation. Also, for the passage of laws that will protect the public

39. Frederick C. Howe, *Wisconsin: An Experiment in Democracy* (New York 1912), p. 164; C. A. Lyman, "The Cooperative Society in Wisconsin," in National Conference on Marketing and Farm Credits, *Marketing and Farm Credits, 191.* (Madison, Wis., 1916), pp. 41–42.

by placing officials who will authorize and permit such useless waste of the people's money in the institutions at Mendota [the state insane asylum] or Waupun [the state penitentiary]." A few months earlier, when students preparing for the consular service petitioned the university authorities for courses in Chinese and Japanese, the Equity publication demanded that the requests be turned down. These were "special" and purely "personal professions," it held, "from which the general public will derive no benefit whatever."[40]

Finally in 1914, the state board of public affairs, much to the satisfaction of the Equity authorities, began an investigation of the university, including the college of agriculture. The resulting *Survey of the University of Wisconsin*, whatever the animus which inspired its compilers, contained much valuable information and gave a clear insight into the thinking of various groups. It set forth the facts concerning the teaching of agricultural economics and rural problems, including marketing. It pointed out, deprecatingly, that the Wisconsin college of agriculture was "more than forty years old before it began to teach the distribution and marketing of farm wealth in general, and to study Wisconsin market problems in particular." These facts could not be disputed, but it was also true that the Wisconsin college of agriculture was one of the few such institutions in the nation to offer courses in agricultural economics at all.[41]

The state board, in the course of its investigations, found that many times the college authorities held opinions at variance with the "definite" and "positive" demands of certain farmer groups. It admitted, however, that the college staff "opposed" or "held aloof" from many such proposals because they were deemed "violative of economic, social or civic law." It conceded also that the farmers' complaints were "apt to be crude, unwise, and ineffective in the proposed principles and methods of action."

The college cannot be expected to head an agrarian revolution for distributive justice. If it were proper to do so, it is beyond reason to expect it. It is not recorded in history that fat men, lawyers, and college professors ever headed a

40. *Wisconsin Equity News*, May 10, 1908, p. 6; August 10, 1909, p. 10; August 25, 1909, p. 5.

41. *Report upon the Survey of the University of Wisconsin: Findings of the State Board of Public Affairs and its Report to the Legislature* (Madison, [1915]), pp. 942–45.

riot. Teachers are conservative by nature, with courage very like that of Burns' field mouse. . . . [The college] cannot be allied with farm organizations or devote itself to class propagandism; but it can put freely at the service of students, farmers, farm leaders and their organizations the knowledge that is needed for wise action.[42]

No doubt all this Equity pressure had some effect. For example, the Wisconsin college of agriculture presently took pains to study the history of cheese from producer to consumer, and the state board of control formulated plans for a more efficient system of marketing.[43]

The Equity Society, besides putting pressure on the college of agriculture, also exerted influence on the state legislature. The first major legislative measure to attract the attention of the organization was a bill seeking additional funds to build and maintain a state-owned binder-twine plant which was expected not only to manufacture twine for the farmers at lower prices but also to net the state a profit. A bill providing the necessary funds for such a plant was introduced in the legislature of 1909, but, much to the disgust of the Equity leadership, it was defeated. This was enough to grind the wheels of discontent, and Theodore Roosevelt's words, "Farmers Must Organize," became suddenly popular. A thorough analysis of the strength of Equity influence in the Wisconsin legislature brought out the fact that the assemblymen in and adjoining the organized Equity territory voted for the binder-twine bill, while those in and around the unorganized territory voted against it.[44]

That Equity was also interested in other progressive measures is evident from the demands it made during the state election campaign of 1910. The Wisconsin society favored more stringent education laws; completion of the binder-twine plant; conservation of natural resources; enactment of employers' liability and industrial insurance; establishment of a state commission to study living costs and the difference between the prices received by the farmers and those paid by the consumers; encouragement of coöperative buying and selling; extension of the scope and authority of the dairy and food commission; improvements in the registration, primary

42. *Ibid.*, pp. 947–49.

43. R. W. Campbell, "Coöperation in Wisconsin," *American Review of Reviews,* XLVII (April, 1913), p. 470.

44. Wisconsin State Board of Control, *Biennial Report,* 1911–12, pp. 10–11; *Wisconsin Equity News,* July 25, 1909, pp. 4–7; *ibid.,* June 10, 1909, p. 10.

and general election laws; passage of a corrupt practices act and initiative, referendum, and recall measures; and the sale of the remaining public lands to actual settlers on long-term contracts.[45]

The Wisconsin legislature of 1911 was one of the most remarkable in the history of the state. Included among its long list of progressive accomplishments were measures providing for an industrial commission, workmen's compensation, state life insurance, an income tax, limitations on the labor of women and children, a state binder-twine plant, a cooperative-marketing law, and a state board of public affairs. Highly gratified with the accomplishments of the session, the *Wisconsin Equity News* boasted that the legislature had fulfilled its platform pledge to the farmers; and the following year the executive board of the order announced that in the past two years Equity had received more political recognition than ever before.[46]

The Wisconsin Society of Equity was not content with a merely political program; it was also active in promoting the organization of local cooperative associations. It helped create the Sheboygan County Cheese Producers' Federation, later known as the Wisconsin Cheese Producers' Federation, although a Plymouth farmer named Henry Krumery, who only later became a member of Equity, was mainly responsible for its growth.[47] But perhaps the biggest Equity accomplishment was the organization of local cooperative livestock-shipping associations. The first of these was organized at Durand in 1906, but the years of greatest activity along this line came during the period from 1912 to 1916. Individual associations began business with approximately thirty members; but in well-organized areas such as Pierce County, membership lists included as many as three or four hundred farmers. In 1917, the Ellsworth Equity Cooperative Association reported 520 members and claimed to be the largest in the state.[48]

45. *Ibid.*, September 25, 1910, pp. 9–10.

46. Milo M. Quaife, *Wisconsin, Its History and Its People, 1634–1924* (2 vols., Chicago, 1924), II, 36; *Wisconsin Equity News,* June 25, 1911, pp. 4–5; *ibid.,* October 25, 1912, p. 1; National Conference on Marketing and Farm Credits, *Marketing and Farm Credits,* pp. 39–40; Edwin G. Nourse, *Legal Status of Agricultural Cooperation* (New York, 1927), p. 46.

47. *Equity News,* September 1, 1915, p. 129; Henry Krumery, *A Blow at the Cheese Trust* (n.p., n.d.), pp. 7–8 [pamphlet].

48. Edwin G. Nourse and Joseph G. Knapp, *Co-Operative Marketing of Live-*

While the Equity Society was entrenching itself in Wisconsin, the spring wheat growers were beginning to organize under its leadership in Minnesota, the Dakotas, and then in Montana. This was accomplished mainly through the Equity Cooperative Exchange, the first cooperative terminal marketing agency of importance in the United States. Later, a livestock-marketing firm was added. Generally speaking, the organizers of the exchange operated on the theory that local cooperative marketing reform, desirable as it was, did not and could not provide relief from the abuses that existed on the terminal market.[49]

The grievances of the spring wheat growers against the grain merchants were of long standing, and when Equity projected itself into the struggle it simply followed in the footsteps of the Grangers, the Alliancemen, the Populists, and other promoters of the cooperative grain-marketing movement. In graphic style Equity leaders denounced the grain merchants for depressing prices, underweighing, undergrading, and heavily assessing the farmers for foreign material in their grain. The mixing of lower-grade wheat with that of a higher grade and selling the mixed wheat as the higher grade was termed a fraud. The railroads, the bankers, and the Minnesota State Grading and Inspection Board were considered enemies of the farmers.[50] The railroads were charged with both denying cars when needed and exacting heavy tolls when the cars were furnished. The bankers and other agencies financing the movement of grain were "usurers." The Minnesota State Grading and Inspection Board was assailed as the tool of "speculators," "grain gamblers," "vultures," "pilferers," "bandits," "pirates," "thieves," "crooks," and "the Grain Combine." All this, when reduced to the smallest common denominator, became the

---

stock (Washington, 1931), pp. 12–16; B. H. Hibbard and Asher Hobson, "Cooperation in Wisconsin," University of Wisconsin Agricultural Experiment Station, Bulletin 282 (Madison, 1917), p. 17; Equity News, May 1, 1917, p. 10.

49. For a statement by the head of the Equity Cooperative Exchange explaining why farmers had taken to the terminal market, see the Equity Farm News (Fargo, N. Dak.), January 1, 1912, p. 13.

50. L. D. H. Weld, "Cooperation in Minnesota," Papers and Proceedings of the Seventh Annual Meeting of the Minnesota Academy of the Social Sciences (Minneapolis, 1914), VII, 57–58; Report of the Federal Trade Commission on the Grain Trade (7 vols., Washington, 1920–1926), III, 154–61 [see page 161 for the argument of the grain trade]; Minnesota Leader (Olivia), December 17, 31, 1921.

Minneapolis Chamber of Commerce, which to many grain growers was the perfect symbol of graft and corruption.[51]

To evaluate fairly the charges and countercharges made by the farmers and the grain trade is no simple task. Much of the printed material is highly emotional. Granted that many charges were probably true, others exaggerated, and still others half true, the fact is that many farmers believed the charges. Because of this, they readily joined first the Equity Cooperative Exchange and then later the Nonpartisan League. As so frequently noted, what people believe to be true is often more important than the truth itself.

The mere launching of an attack against the Minneapolis Chamber of Commerce, which to the farmers was a monopoly, greatly accelerated the growth of the exchange in the northwestern grain-growing area. Here La Follette was popular and the progressive movement was strong. George S. Loftus, James A. Manahan, Benjamin Drake, and Magnus Johnson, influential leaders with the exchange at one time or another, represented varying shades of the progressive viewpoint in politics. *La Follette's Magazine* published numerous articles favorable to the exchange marketing program, while Equity publications gave much space to La Follette. Thus the exchange represented something broader than mere terminal marketing reform.[52]

The marketing program of Equity was aided, no doubt, by the presence of large numbers of Scandinavians in the spring wheat area. The Scandinavian Transportation Company, organized during the late 1860's, was

51. *Equity Farm News,* December 1, 1911, p. 15; *Interstate Commerce Commission Reports* (Washington, 1908), XII, 563–64; *Montana Equity News* (Great Falls), September 14, 1916; W. E. Davis, "Fighting the Grain Combine," *La Follette's Magazine* (Madison, Wis.), VI (January 17, 1914), p. 3; *La Follette's Magazine,* V (December 13, 1913), p. 5; *ibid.* (December 20, 1913), p. 5; *Equity Cooperative Exchange, Proposed Farmers' Terminal Elevator, St. Paul, Minnesota* (n.p., n.d.), inside back cover; Charles E. Russell, "The Revolt of the Farmers," *Pearson's Magazine,* XXXIII (April, 1915), pp. 417–27; *Coöperators' Herald* (Fargo, N. Dak.), October 24, 1913; March 6, August 7, 1914. For a more critical account of the financing of grain shipments by bankers and commission firms, see F.T.C., *The Grain Trade,* III, 183–96.

52. *The New International Year Book,* 1912, p. 476. La Follette won the first presidential primary election in North Dakota in 1912. Somewhat typical were the remarks appearing in the *Coöperators' Herald* for March 6, 1914, and July 23, 1915.

probably the first cooperative marketing organization in Minnesota. There is reason to believe that during the Equity period more cooperative stores creameries, and elevators existed among the Scandinavians of the North west than among the native Americans. Among the Scandinavians progres sive views in politics were also strong.[53]

Significantly, Equity sentiment had penetrated into the Edmonton Alberta, area as early as 1905, but had made slight headway there becaus the Canadian farmers were reluctant to affiliate with a strictly American organization. The grain growers of western Canada, however, with griev ances similar to those suffered south of the border, had appealed to their government for aid and had obtained substantial assistance in the estab lishment of cooperative elevators. All this was watched with the greates interest by the American farmers, who made it a point to compare the prices obtained by the Canadian cooperatives at Winnipeg with the price paid for grain in Minneapolis. Whenever higher prices prevailed in Winnipeg, the natural assumption was that the attitude of the Canadian government made the difference, and Equity enthusiasts placed the blam for the lower prices paid on the Minneapolis market on the Minneapoli Chamber of Commerce.[54] Whether the facts warranted such an assump tion is beside the point. The Equity farmers believed it to be true.

The immediate forerunner of the Equity Cooperative Exchange was the short-lived Minnesota Farmers' Exchange, the spring wheat counterpar of an abortive national movement for reform on the terminal markets The Minnesota exchange, established in 1902, was incorporated fo $500,000, but speedily found that it could not hope to dispose of any grain it might obtain without a seat on the Minneapolis Chamber o Commerce. But all efforts by the exchange to purchase a seat on the cham ber proved futile. Chamber representatives claimed that membership wa denied the exchange on grounds of insolvency, a charge which the ex change leaders heatedly denied. And so the Minnesota Farmers' Exchang accomplished nothing, except to build up farmer sentiment against th

53. Larson, *The Wheat Market,* p. 104; Edward A. Ross, *The Old World in th New* (New York, 1914), p. 91.

54. Louis A. Wood, *A History of Farmer Movements in Canada* (Toronto, 1924) pp. 199-201; Harald S. Patton, *Grain Growers' Cooperation in Western Canad* (Cambridge, Mass., 1928), pp. 114-17; *Hearings on Grain Exchanges* (63 Con gress, 2 session, House Resolution 424, Washington, 1915), pp. 180-91.

chamber. All this information was at the disposal of the Equity representatives who assembled in Minneapolis on May 30, 1908, to organize the Equity Cooperative Exchange.[55]

There were other preliminaries. The first phase of Equity operations in the northwest probably began on May 25, 1903, with the circulation of Everitt's series of "Dollar Wheat Bulletins" urging farmers to withhold their wheat from market until the price of one dollar per bushel could be obtained. Many northwestern farmers accepted this advice, and when necessary even constructed new warehouses and granaries in which to store their wheat. Much to their joy they found that the price of wheat did rise to the dollar level, a development for which Equity leaders immediately assumed full credit. Next year Equity sponsored another "hold-your-wheat" campaign, but without the favorable results claimed in 1903. Other similar attempts followed, and in 1907, according to Equity statistics, some thirty million bushels of wheat had been pledged; but the program as a whole was a failure. The chief obstacles to success were the futility of the plan, poor leadership, dissension at national headquarters, and the lack of a satisfactory method for the financing of pooling members. Despite these failures, the hold-your-wheat program was not altogether without results. By recruiting ten or twelve thousand Equity members in North Dakota alone, the leaders of the movement had paved the way for the much more important program of cooperative marketing.[56]

With the organization of the Equity Cooperative Exchange in 1908, the grain-marketing program in the Northwest entered its second phase. The "grain growers' division" of the American Society of Equity had plans to organize the grain growers of the country on as many terminal markets as possible, but it was only in the spring wheat country that the program materialized. By this time it was abundantly clear that organizing local farm associations and establishing state service and educational organizations to aid the farmers in cleaning, grading, and storing their grain were not enough. Much as these achievements might improve local marketing

55. Co-operators' Guide (Indianapolis), IV (February, 1911), p. 4.
56. Nash, in World Today, XIII (July, 1907), p. 717; Chelsa C. Sherlock, The Modern Farm Cooperative (Des Moines, 1922), pp. 14–15; Equity Farm Journal, (May, 1908), p. 10; Devils Lake (N. Dak.) Inter-Ocean, June 28, 1907; Hibbard, Marketing Agricultural Products, pp. 232–33; Herman Steen, Coöperative Marketing (New York, 1923), p. 212.

conditions, they did nothing toward the reform of conditions on the terminal market. What was needed was a farmers' terminal marketing firm that would receive grain shipped on consignment, or, better still, could be fed by a chain of local cooperatives with ample storage facilities. With such a setup the farmers could clean, condition, transfer, and store their grain at a minimum of risk and expense, and thus retain control of their grain from the time it left the farm until it was sold on the terminal market.[57]

The exchange marketing program was significant in that it sought to organize the farmers on the basis of the crop produced. By so doing its leaders were pursuing a realistic course, for experience had revealed that the "farming class" was a heterogeneous group consisting of farmers with differing and frequently antagonistic interests and that the success of a marketing organization depended primarily on bringing together producers of the same crops who had the same problems. The farmers could also, should the need be felt, organize as consumers to purchase feed, seeds, fertilizers, machinery, farm implements, and general farm supplies.[58]

Unfortunately, such a plan of organization was hardly designed to promote good relations between the American Society of Equity and the Equity Cooperative Exchange. Sharp differences developed between the parent order and its offspring over aims and objectives, policies, jurisdiction, and finances. The Equity Cooperative Exchange was interested solely in the problems of the spring wheat grower, while the American Society of Equity claimed an interest in all farmers—"the grain grower, the stock feeder, the dairyman, the tobacco grower, the fruit grower, the cotton grower." The exchange was realistic and opportunistic, while the Equity Society was idealistic and altruistic. The former saw no reason why it should submit to policies that did not directly and immediately benefit the grain producers, while the latter asked that commodity and regional interests be submerged for the general welfare of the farmers as a class.

57. *Coöperators' Herald*, October 10, 1913, and April 17, 1914; *Equity Farm News*, January 1, 1912, p. 13. See Lionel Smith-Gordon, *Cooperation for Farmers* (London, 1918), pp. 190–93, for a good, brief discussion on the pros and cons of local and terminal marketing operations.

58. George Harold Powell, *Coöperation in Agriculture* (New York, 1913), pp. 5–10, 18–23; Chris L. Christensen, *Farmers' Cooperative Associations in the United States. 1929*, U. S. Dept. Agri., Circular 94 (Washington, 1929).

These conflicting philosophies were responsible for many of the rifts and cleavages within Equity ranks.[59]

Although the exchange was organized in 1908, it was not until 1911 that it was incorporated under the laws of North Dakota for the purchase and sale of grain on consignment. Its executives included John M. Anderson, former member of the North Dakota legislature who headed the exchange until 1922, as president; A. A. Trovatten, a grain solicitor, employed to drum up business; and Pliney E. Cooper as agent and sales manager. The sales of the exchange were small between the years 1908 and 1912, amounting to only 805 cars for the period, and out of these, 681 were reportedly sold through members of the Minneapolis Chamber of Commerce. Cooper's services with the exchange ended on August 1, 1912, when George S. Loftus became sales manager. This marked the beginning of the third and perhaps the most spectacular phase in the history of the exchange.[60]

Loftus was more a reformer than a business manager. He came to the exchange as an aggressive and uncompromising foe of the organized grain trade and as a seasoned campaigner for La Follette progressivism. He hardly fitted the requirement of an expert trained in the principles and practices of cooperative marketing. His chief qualification was that, in season and out of season, he fought for and represented the point of view of the small shipper. Like the farmers among whom he worked, Loftus was a great admirer of Senator La Follette. He was an artful platform speaker, and his mastery of farmer psychology brought farmers from miles around to hear him denounce the "grain combine." Naturally Loftus was cordially hated by the organized grade trade, which regarded his elevation to office as tantamount to a declaration of war against the Minneapolis Chamber of Commerce.[61]

59. *Plan of the American Society of Equity,* p. 20; Everitt, *The Third Power,* third edition, p. 277; *Equity Farm Journal,* I (December, 1907), p. 4; (May, 1908), p. 5.

60. House Resolution 424, 63 Congress, 2 session, p. 340; C. U. Pierson, *The American Society of Equity* (Casselton, N. Dak., 1909), pp. 1–2 [pamphlet]; *State of North Dakota Legislative Manual,* 1907, p. 370; *Federal Trade Commission Decisions* (Washington, 1926), VII, 145.

61. Equity Cooperative Exchange, *Cooperation in Marketing of Grain* (Minneapolis, n.d.) [pamphlet].

Meanwhile, the chamber of commerce had been maintaining a vigilant eye over the activities of the exchange and had been girding itself for future action. There were some merchants who believed that the exchange, if allowed to go on unchecked, would provide the nucleus for a powerful cooperative movement. The thing to do, therefore, was to destroy it in its infancy. This task was assigned to John G. McHugh, secretary of the Minneapolis Chamber of Commerce, a man who had been associated previously with the Winnipeg Board of Trade and had been active against the Canadian cooperatives. Undoubtedly the decision to turn McHugh loose against the exchange was a mistake from the point of view of the chamber of commerce, for it was all that was needed to spur the Equity leaders into action.[62]

The clash between the chamber and the exchange became the subject of a series of legislative inquiries during the session of 1913. A Minnesota house committee, sympathetic with the exchange, began its investigations first; thereupon the grain trade, aroused because of the activities of the house, instigated an investigation by the senate, which reputedly was more favorable to the interests of the private merchants. The public, as a result, was treated to the spectacle of seeing two rival groups seeking to substantiate their known convictions. Neither group conducted an impartial investigation, but each, with some accuracy, accused the other of being unfair.[63]

Early in 1914, Congressman James A. Manahan, the counsel for the Minnesota house committee, introduced a resolution in the national House of Representatives calling for a congressional investigation of the grain trade. The resolution was adopted, and a congressional committee was appointed which included, besides Manahan himself, J. Campbell Cantrill, former president of the Kentucky Society of Equity, and I. L. Lenroot of Wisconsin, whose progressive leanings were already well known. Little,

62. Paul Fossum, *Agrarian Movement in North Dakota* (Baltimore, 1925), p. 83; F.T.C., *Decisions*, VII, 145.

63. *Minnesota Journal of the House*, 1913, pp. 1748–57; House Resolution 424, 63 Congress, 2 session, pp. 397–401; *Minnesota Journal of the Senate*, 1913, pp. 231, 285. For a newspaper account of the senate and house committee investigations, see the scrapbook of Benjamin Drake, in the private possession of Benjamin Drake of Minneapolis.

if anything, came from this probe other than a considerable amount of publicity for the exchange.[64]

By late 1914 the exchange had plunged into the campaign to erect a state-owned terminal elevator in North Dakota, a campaign which dated back to the days of the Farmers' Alliance and the Populists. The elevator issue was put to a popular vote in 1912 and again in 1914. Each time it passed with a decided majority. Legislation also had been enacted for the financing of the project, while the state board of control had been authorized to investigate the subject and to present plans to the legislature for the building of the state elevator.[65]

The board of control began its investigations by visiting terminal elevators in the United States and Canada and interviewing government officials, grain merchants, bankers, business leaders, and cooperative leaders. Among those consulted were representatives of the Minneapolis Chamber of Commerce, the Duluth Board of Trade, and the Equity Cooperative Exchange. But instead of presenting plans as it had been ordered to do, the board of control became critical of the project. It recommended strongly against the state's erecting such an elevator and advised that if the state insisted on doing something of the sort, it would be better to lease an elevator and try out the scheme at the lowest possible cost.[66]

The exchange, in anticipation of the unfavorable report, prepared a lengthy statement of its own to present to the North Dakota legislature, and in cooperation with other Equity groups it called a mass meeting of farmers to assemble in Bismarck at the time the board of control was to make its recommendations. The exchange statement criticized the board for failing to interview people who were best qualified to present the Equity point of view. It defended participation by the exchange in the controversy on the ground that it was a North Dakota corporation, 90 per cent of whose members paid taxes to the state. Such an elevator, the ex-

64. J. E. Boyle, "The Agrarian Movement in the Northwest," *American Economic Review*, VIII (September, 1918), p. 513.

65. John D. Hicks, *The Populist Revolt* (Minneapolis, 1931), pp. 287–89; Herbert Gaston, *The Nonpartisan League* (New York, 1920), pp. 40–41; Fossum, *Agrarian Movements in North Dakota*, p. 87; Andrew A. Bruce, *Non-Partisan League* (New York, 1921), p. 57.

66. *North Dakota Journal of the House*, 1915, pp. 165–69.

change claimed, would stimulate competition, bring higher prices, provide farmers with adequate storage facilities, aid them in their cleaning and drying operations, and, in short, provide them with many of the benefits that the Canadian farmers already enjoyed. With the failure of the North Dakota Board of Control to act on the measure, St. Paul became the desirable spot for the location of this elevator because of its strategic situation at the head of the Mississippi River, its admirable transportation facilities, its willingness to contribute to the success of the venture, and its well-established reputation of friendliness to the farmers' cause.[67] The subsequent efforts of the North Dakota farmers to secure a terminal elevator are closely interwoven with the history of the Nonpartisan League, and will be considered in the next chapter.

The bitter campaigns in behalf of a terminal elevator which the Equity Society was waging in North Dakota against the Minneapolis Chamber of Commerce no doubt helped the organization to spread westward into Montana. This state lies beyond the boundary of the western Middle West, but since in its farming activities it was becoming a kind of projection of North Dakota, its interest in the Equity Society is worth noting briefly. Montana, in 1914, was still a booming pioneer state about to complete the transition from a cattle-raising to a grain-growing economy Rising grain prices and bumper crops promised to make grain growing a veritable bonanza. Montana's prospects had lured thousands of immigrants from the Dakotas, Minnesota, Canada, and other grain-growing areas. With easy credit provided by eastern mortgage companies and middle western bankers, loan agents were familiar people. So, too, were automobile and tractor salesmen. New towns, churches, schools, and road appeared. Land values soared, and so did debts; but the favorable climate the breaking of much fresh sod, and the European war helped many to conclude that prosperity had come to stay.[68]

The influx of new population, together with bumper crops and high wheat prices, which enabled farmers to pay dues, accounted largely for

67. *Ibid.*, pp. 932–35; *Pioneer Press* (St. Paul), February 3, 4, 1915; *Bismarc Daily Tribune,* January 31, 1915.

68. Bureau of Agriculture, Labor and Industry, *Montana Resources and Oppc tunities* (Helena, 1933), p. 75; *Coöperators' Herald,* July 23, 1915; *Montana R sources and Opportunities,* pp. 74–75.

the rapid growth of the Montana Equity from a membership of 200 in 1914 to 6,000 in 1916. By 1917 the *Montana Equity News* claimed 12,000 subscribers, 60,000 readers, and an Equity membership of about 15,000.[69]

The complaints of the Montana farmers were similar to those of their neighbors in Canada, Minnesota, and the Dakotas. They had also watched with interest the campaigns of the Canadian growers and those of the Equity Cooperative Exchange. Many of the newly arrived settlers had belonged to the Equity Society in the older states to the east or to the co-operative organizations in Canada to the north. Oddly enough, the Montanans seemed to display a greater interest in the Canadian movement than they did in the exchange.[70]

Besides protesting against the unfavorable wheat market, Montana farmers also registered complaints against the high cost of farm supplies and consumer goods and the dominating influence of the mining corporations in the state government. To fight against these conditions Equity promoted the establishment of cooperative marketing and purchasing associations, consumer stores, and cooperative credit and insurance companies; it agitated for lower railroad rates and a reformed tax system, and finally it undertook a persistent courtship of organized labor. But most of this activity was in vain. Successive crop failures, factionalism, declining wheat prices, and the postwar reaction eventually placed the Montana Equity in its grave. By 1918 it had yielded its leadership as a farm order to the Nonpartisan League.[71]

During and immediately following World War I, the activities of the Wisconsin Society of Equity and the Equity Cooperative Exchange were apparently headed for newer and loftier heights, but this appearance was

69. *Montana Equity News*, February 23, March 22, July 19, 1917; *Great Falls Tribune*, June 15, 1917.

70. Patton, *Grain Growers' Cooperation in Western Canada*, pp. 114–17; *Montana Equity News*, February 22, November 15, 1917; April 25, 1918; J. M. Mehl, *Cooperative Grain Marketing*, U. S. Dept. Agri., Bulletin 937 (Washington, 1921), p. 1–5.

71. *Montana Equity News*, August 24, 1916; January 4, 11, March 1, 1917; *Nonpartisan Leader* (Fargo, N. Dak.), January 28, 1916, p. 4; *Great Falls Tribune*, January 10, February 18, May 16, 1917; Louis Levine, *The Taxation of Mines in Montana* (New York, 1919), pp. 10–14; *The Nation*, CVII (November 2, 1918), p. 507–8; *Montana Equity News*, May 24, August 16, 1917; May 2, 1918; August 0, 1919.

illusory. In point of fact these two remaining segments of Equity strength were soon to founder on the rocks of disaster.

In Wisconsin, the demand for direct political action surpassed the earlier enthusiasm for cooperatives. Early in 1917 the Nonpartisan League had attracted the attention of some of the politically minded members of the Wisconsin Society of Equity. On March 22 about two hundred farmers representing eighteen counties assembled in Marshfield and, after marked differences over the best methods of organization, finally decided to demand immediate affiliation of the Equity with the League. Another meeting held in Wausau the same year indicated that a well-groomed political machine would be ready for the elections of 1918.[72]

Chief aspirant for the leadership of the political movement was James N. Tittemore, already three times an unsuccessful candidate for Congress. Despite the avocational character of his farming activities, he spoke eloquently and profusely of the need for "farmers to represent farmers," and presented himself as one ideally qualified to lead the "soil-tilling fraternity" to victory. Tittemore set for himself the task of getting 50,000 members for the Wisconsin Equity, and by combining rhetoric, politics, religion, and sophistry, he came close to attaining his goal. He spoke of Lincoln and his efforts to preserve the American homestead, of his own birth in a log cabin, of his rise from telegraph boy to traffic manager of a railroad, of how the farmers were being "skinned" by the railroads, and of the hope for emancipating the farmers by taking to direct political action. This ushered in one of the most uproarious periods in the history of the organization.[73]

Rumors of a farmer-labor alignment assumed new proportions in 191? after an announcement to the effect that the Nonpartisan League would not present a slate until two years later. An organization, temporarily known as the Wisconsin Farmers' Progressive League, called a meeting for May 1 to decide on the platform, the candidates, and the party through which the new political alliance was to function. Enthusiasts sought to

72. *Wisconsin Leader* (Madison), September 11, 1920; *Equity News,* March 1917, pp. 720, 726; *Organized Farmer* (Milwaukee), April 26, 1917, p. 5.

73. *Evening Wisconsin* (Milwaukee), May 2, 1918; *Equity News,* January 1918, p. 259.

allay the fears of the apprehensive by the argument that "conditions are now different." [74]

On May 1 approximately five hundred delegates representing Equity, the Nonpartisan League, and organized labor met in Madison to nominate a slate headed by Tittemore. Merlin Hull and John J. Blaine, both prominent in progressive circles, were nominated for secretary of state and attorney general, respectively. These endorsements were made without party designation.[75]

The *Milwaukee Leader,* the daily Socialist publication, suspicious of the Madison gathering, sent a special representative to determine the motives behind the meeting. According to his report, certain prominent Equity men were the "guiding spirits" in the movement, and the meeting was merely the beginning of a drive to place Tittemore in the governor's chair. Tittemore was accused of willingness to use any party to satisfy his ambitions and even of appropriating his platform from the "immediate demands" of the Socialist party in order to bait it with "a program, luscious and appetizing." [76]

Like the La Follette reformers before them, the Tittemore supporters decided to cast their lot with the Republican party. But they pushed their program and their candidates in every part of the state. The *National Equity News* helped the cause along by filling its pages with campaign promises. Whether Tittemore had completely alienated himself from the political affections of the Nonpartisan League is uncertain, but he did try to capitalize on what League sentiment existed in the state. But all this was in vain. Tittemore was defeated in the Republican primaries by the incumbent, Emanuel Philipp, who got 72,000 votes against 45,000 for the "ambitious Equitarian." In the general elections, only John J. Blaine, the nominee for attorney general, was elected.[77]

Shortly after this election, the Wisconsin Equity became involved in

74. *Milwaukee Daily News,* April 6, 1918; *National Equity News* (Madison, Wis.), April 18, 1918, pp. 1, 7.

75. *Organized Farmer,* May 30, 1918, p. 9; *National Equity News,* May 2, 1918, p. 4.

76. *Milwaukee Leader,* May 3, 1918.

77. *National Equity News,* September 12, 1918, pp. 6–7; *Blue Book of the State of Wisconsin,* 1919, p. 93.

internecine warfare. The year 1919 found the state and national organizations embroiled in controversies over postwar issues, politics, and finances. The Red issue also was injected into the struggles and dissensions.[78] Despite the numerous factions, however, the aggressive Tittemore prepared to seek the Republican nomination for governor again in 1920. But this time the Nonpartisan League entered the campaign with a ticket of its own in reality a La Follette progressive slate under new political clothing. The League lost no time in exposing the political machinations of Tittemore, who had urged it to organize in Wisconsin and had then turned against it to satisfy his own interests. The League ticket, incidentally, was headed by John J. Blaine, who had been elected attorney general on the Tittemore ticket in 1918.[79]

Once again Tittemore waged an aggressive campaign, and once again he was defeated. This time he received only a little more than half as many votes as in 1918, while of the six candidates for the nomination, he received the fewest votes. He failed even to secure the votes of the Equity members and their families, upon which he had so greatly relied. From this time on his activities in the Equity became negligible; in fact, his exit was about as hurried as was his entrance.[80]

The successor of Tittemore to the state presidency of the Wisconsin Society of Equity was E. C. Pommerening, Tittemore's first lieutenant. Functioning after the fashion of his master, this youthful would-be administrator supplanted the Tittemore mania for politics with his own mania for cooperatives, setting up enterprises with a fantastic swiftness that sapped the organization of its remaining strength. Placing a ranking official on a political ticket and using Equity resources to promote his candidacy was bad enough, but the promotion of a succession of cooperative failures was even worse. Pommerening's policy brought down upon the society the rising wrath of the older members and furnished the opposition with a much-appreciated opportunity to denounce it as a racket

78. *Wisconsin Equity News*, November 27, 1919, p. 9.

79. *Wisconsin Leader*, November 6, 1920; *Organized Farmer*, September 1920, p. 20.

80. *Ibid.*, p. 2.

81. *Equity News*, December 15, 1920, p. 8; December 22, 1920, p. 3; *Wisconsin Leader*, January 29, 1921; *Wisconsin State Journal* (Madison), October 21, November 29, 1921; *Capital Times* (Madison), November 4, 1921.

Equally turbulent was the course pursued by the Equity Cooperative Exchange. Much of the crusading fervor of the exchange subsided after its departure from Minneapolis in 1914, and this, coupled with the rising wartime demands for farm products, brought a growth in its business activities. In 1914, it organized the St. Paul Grain Exchange, a "non-stock membership corporation" that was expected to become a sort of farmer-managed and controlled chamber of commerce.[82]

The St. Paul Grain Exchange required that all grain be sold through its members, who in turn charged a commission of one cent a bushel to sellers and shippers. Buyers, however, could make use of its facilities without purchasing through a broker and without having to pay a commission. This, exchange leaders said, made St. Paul an open market. The Equity Cooperative Exchange held two seats on the St. Paul Grain Exchange.[83]

In 1916, the exchange expanded its activities into livestock marketing, then into wool marketing, and finally into the cooperative purchasing of farm supplies. It entered the livestock-marketing field on the South St. Paul market. Its leaders had become convinced that the successes experienced in organizing local cooperative associations in Wisconsin, Minnesota, and upper Iowa warranted expansion into the terminal market. This move was noteworthy for two reasons: first, this was the forerunner of a series of similar commodity organizations sponsored by the Farmers' Union, the Farm Bureau, and numerous independent groups in the Middle West; and second, it brought to a head a standing controversy among the several Equity organizations on the policy of terminal marketing. The question at issue was whether farmers should continue to endorse those private terminal firms which had handled the livestock of the local associations in the past, or whether they should give their exclusive support to a farmer-owned and controlled agency. The establishment of the terminal agency indicated the predominance of the latter view.[84]

Business began on the South St. Paul market in October, 1916, and two years later a branch was established in Chicago. However, events soon

82. F.T.C., *Decisions*, VII, 137.

83. *Non-partisan Leader*, August 17, 1916, p. 6; *Minnesota Leader*, October 9, 1920.

84. Nourse and Knapp, *The Co-Operative Marketing of Livestock*, pp. 12–14, 16–7; *Organized Farmer*, January 24, 1919, p. 10.

convinced even the most enthusiastic exchange supporters that their ter
minal livestock-marketing operations were either ill advised or misman
aged, or both.[85]

The war years witnessed a rapid growth in the grain business of th
exchange. New elevators were built or acquired, the number of stock
holders was increased, and the financial reports presented favorable ac
counts of the progress of the organization. By midyear of 1922, the ex
change owned eighty local elevators—fifty-two in North Dakota, two i
South Dakota, and twenty-six in Minnesota. The exchange also operate
twelve local cooperative elevators for farmer groups that either were un
able financially to operate themselves or else preferred to operate as par
of a large marketing organization.[86]

The stockholders' report for 1922 hinted that the financial conditio
of the exchange was not so healthy as previously claimed. Then, in th
following year, the ugly rumors that circulated were confirmed. Th
capital stock of the exchange had been impaired to the extent of $750,000
money that had been obtained from the sale of the grain in the pool c
1923 had been diverted to the general business of the exchange; and
substantial amount of pool money had not been paid to the stockholder
Some fifteen elevators were located in territory that was not essentiall
grain-producing.[87]

Poor business leadership was the most important single reason for th
decline of the exchange. Beginning with the time when one of its ma
agers did not know enough to keep his personal accounts separate fro
those of the company, through the period when the business policies
the exchange had oscillated between "applied Christianity" and progre
sivism in politics, down into the unhealthy expansion of the war perio
the history of the exchange was one long procession of errors.

Psychologically also the management of the exchange was handicappe

85. *Equity News,* March 1, 1915, p. 714.

86. *Montana Equity News,* April 17, 1919; Ralph L. Harmon to Austin P. Hain
September 9, 1919, in the possession of R. L. Harmon of South St. Paul. See al
H. B. Price, "Farmers' Cooperation in Minnesota, 1917–1922," *University of Minn
sota Agricultural Experiment Station, Bulletin* 202 (St. Paul, 1923), p. 35.

87. Equity Cooperative Exchange, *Statement by the Board of Directors* (Farg
N. Dak., 1922), p. 3; Equity Cooperative Exchange, *Twelfth Annual Stockhold
Convention, January 16–17–18, 1923.*

Its leadership was composed of agitators who were ill prepared for business management. It was more interested in war against the Minneapolis Chamber of Commerce than in the adoption of sound business policies. Resistance against the attacks of the chamber of commerce was easy, but the creation of an alternative marketing system was hard. The livestock agency was operated inefficiently; frequently complaints were registered about the poor handling of grain; sales were entrusted to subordinates while the leaders were busy quarreling with one another or else were attending to other matters than business. All this, coupled with the depression which hit the farmers in the early twenties, sent the organization sagging. In 1923, the exchange was finally placed in the hands of receivers, but not without challenge on the part of those who believed that with better management it could have kept going.[88]

The Equity suffered from the fact that it was a loosely knit, in fact regional, organization; only in the period from 1902 to 1907, when the control of the society was vested in Everitt, was there any trace of a central authority. At various intervals its strength was concentrated in Kentucky and Tennessee, Wisconsin, the Dakotas, Minnesota, and Montana. Its greatest strength was gained in Wisconsin, although the extent of the marketing operations of the Equity Cooperative Exchange cannot be overlooked. The influence of the national body never was strong; for the most part, it only struggled to keep itself alive. It would be a mistake to assume that Equity ever at any time acquired the status of a national movement. Eventually the Farmers' Union absorbed the remnants of the Equity, first in the agricultural Northwest and finally in Wisconsin.

But in spite of its unfortunate experiences, Equity left its mark. Under its leadership numerous local grain- and livestock-shipping associations were created, and the farmers were taught the need for a more efficient handling of their produce. Some of its leaders became identified with the Nonpartisan League and took an important part in the League's work, and men like Myron W. Thatcher and others who later assumed positions of leadership in the strong cooperatives built by the Farmers' Union in

88. *St. Paul Daily News,* October 4, 7, 1922; *Courier-News* (Fargo, N. Dak.), January 19, 1923; *Fargo Forum,* February 10, 1923. See also File 150484, *Emil Piper et al.* v. *Equity Cooperative Exchange,* Ramsey County Courthouse, St. Paul, Minn.

the upper Mississippi Valley obtained much of their early training with the old Equity Cooperative Exchange. It was upon the ruins of this last agency that the business program of the Farmers' Union was built. Equity agitated, sometimes successfully, for better grading standards, better warehousing, and better credit facilities; it brought pressure to bear on educational and governmental agencies to devote more attention to problems of marketing and distribution.

Chapter VI

THE NONPARTISAN LEAGUE
BEGINNINGS[1]

THE NONPARTISAN LEAGUE was organized in North Dakota in 1915, and was thus a contemporary of the Equity. It differed sharply from the older society in a number of ways: it originated in the region where it was to score its greatest successes; it placed chief emphasis on political as opposed to economic action; and it was deeply influenced by the Socialist movement and by organized labor. Like the Equity, however, it was organized in an era of rising farm prices, and it appealed most to the discontented spring wheat growers who lived in the northern part of the western Middle West. Eventually the League helped decimate the ranks of the Equity, but when the League, in turn, went into a decline, the Farmers' Union, an order more like the Equity than like the League, moved in to fill the vacuum. Throughout these years the example of the Canadian wheat farmers, who had successfully carried their fight against the organized grain trade to a sympathetic government, greatly influenced the action of the American farmers across the border.[2] Mindful, also, of the success with which organized labor waged war against unemploy-

1. This chapter is reprinted in the main from Theodore Saloutos, "The Rise of the Nonpartisan League in North Dakota, 1915-1917," *Agricultural History*, XX (January, 1946), pp. 43-61.

2. Harald S. Patton, *Grain Growers' Cooperation in Western Canada* (Cambridge, Mass., 1928), pp. 114-17; Louis A. Wood, *A History of Farmers' Movements in Canada* (Toronto, 1924), pp. 199-201.

ment, low wages, poor working conditions, and long hours, the North Dakota farmers were moved to adopt similar methods in their struggle against low farm prices, high transportation rates, unfavorable marketing conditions, and monopoly.

It will be recalled that the burning issue in North Dakota politics by the year 1914 had become the farmers' demand, strongly supported by the Equity Society, for a terminal elevator. In this same year, however, Louis B. Hanna, a conservative, had contrived to win the governorship. Hanna had waged his campaign largely in opposition to extravagance in government, and promptly made it clear that he intended at all costs to prevent the erection of the greatly desired terminal elevator.[3] Equity leaders were certain that the governor would have the support of the state board of control, which was scheduled to make a report on the subject, and they feared the legislature would also be hostile. They therefore called the annual convention of the North Dakota Society of Equity to assemble in Bismarck, the capital, at the time early in February, 1915, when the legislature was expected to have the elevator project under consideration.[4] They also extended an invitation to the Farmers' Union, then a comparatively new organization in the state, to take part in the February convention, to fraternize, and to exchange views on questions that confronted the farmers.[5] When this convention met, it came out strongly in favor of a terminal elevator, and its representatives drew up a bill to present to the legislature.[6] Representatives of the city of St. Paul were on hand to inform the farmers that their city would aid them if the elevator were located there. A feature of the convention was the march to the capitol to present the demands of the farmers, most prominent among them being the construction of a state-owned terminal elevator.[7] When the conven-

3. Andrew A. Bruce, *Non-Partisan League* (New York, 1921), pp. 57–58.

4. Herbert E. Gaston, *The Nonpartisan League* (New York, 1920), p. 43; *Bismarck Daily Tribune*, January 31, 1915; *Pioneer Press* (St. Paul), February 3, 4 1915; *Non-partisan Leader* (Fargo, N. Dak.), September 23, 1915, pp. 5–6.

5. *Coöperators' Herald*, January 1, 1915, p. 4. The Union reported charters authorized for forty-two local chapters in North Dakota in 1914. Farmers' Educational and Cooperative Union of America, Tenth Annual Session, September 1–3 1914, *Minutes*, pp. 18–19.

6. *Pioneer Press*, February 5, 1915.

7. *Coöperators' Herald*, February 5, 1915.

tion adjourned, some of the Equity leaders decided to remain in Bismarck until the elevator issue had been decided.

Among the speakers at an Equity rally held the night before the elevator issue came to a final vote was George S. Loftus, the pugnacious sales manager of the Equity Cooperative Exchange and a seasoned campaigner against the organized grain trade. Whether Loftus labored under the pains of an illness that shortly proved fatal or whether he had become unduly embittered because of the unfavorable report of the board of control is unknown, but the effects of his talk were generally conceded to be detrimental to the Equity cause.[8] Like Senator La Follette, whom he admired, Loftus called the roll of the legislature and in vicious and abusive language denounced those who he suspected would vote against the measure. A number of legislators were in the audience, and his acts unquestionably compelled some wavering members to vote against the measure.[9] It was killed in the lower house by a vote of 64 to 40 on the grounds that the state was not in a financial position to support the project.[10] Some Equity followers predicted that they would return two years hence, but the executive committee of the Equity Cooperative Exchange, meeting in Fargo shortly thereafter, voted to proceed with plans to finance an elevator to be owned by Equity farmers, relying on the city of St. Paul for the donation of a site.[11]

Other farm leaders, however, did not acquiesce in the decision of the legislature. The report was that the resentment of the farmers had been growing, stimulated by such accounts as the one shortly circulated to the effect that in the course of the debate over the elevator bill, Treadwell Twitchell, a leading opponent of the measure, had angrily told the farmers to "Go home and slop the hogs!"[12] Twitchell and his associates de-

8. James E. Boyle, "The Agrarian Movement in the Northwest," *American Economic Review*, VIII (September, 1918), p. 513.

9. William Langer, *The Nonpartisan League* (Mandan, N. Dak., 1920), pp. 13–14. See *Bismarck Tribune*, February 14, 1915, for excerpts from North Dakota newspapers denouncing the activities of Loftus prior to the vote on the elevator bill. See also the *Co-operative Manager and Farmer* (Minneapolis), IV (March, 1915), p. 29–33, for hostile accounts of Equity activities.

10. *Pioneer Press,* February 21, 1915.

11. *Ibid.,* February 22, 1915.

12. Gaston, *The Nonpartisan League,* p. 43; Bruce, *Non-Partisan League,* p. 59; Charles Edward Russell, *The Story of the Nonpartisan League* (New York, 1920),

nied the charge, but whether it was true is immaterial; many of the farmers believed it and it spread like wildfire.

Leadership, at least in the beginning stages, has always played an important part in the organization of reform movements.[13] It was a tremendous factor in the origin and development of the Nonpartisan League. The driving force in the new movement was Arthur C. Townley, one of the most gifted farm organizers as well as one of the most colorful personalities in agrarian history. His ability to organize farmers and collect dues had caused many of his adversaries to dub him "After Cash Townley." He had attended the historic Equity convention in February, 1915, but not in the capacity of delegate or leader; no doubt he was contemplating the idea of organizing a farmers' political movement of his own when the psychological moment presented itself.[14] Townley had an interest in the plight of the farmer because he himself had been an unsuccessful farmer and was reputedly in debt to the extent of $100,000. Nor was socialistic talk strange to him, for he had been recruiting members for the Socialist party of North Dakota.

The radicalism of Townley, in all probability, was influenced by the unsettled surroundings in which he found himself. North Dakota was a young state, having been admitted into the Union in 1889, and its many ethnic groups, which were tenacious in their adherence to Old World traditions, made it seem like the polyglot nations of Europe.[15] According to the 1910 census, there were 156,158 foreign-born whites, representing twenty-five nationalities and 27 per cent of the population at the time. An equal number of natives born of foreign parents raised the total foreign element of the state to well over 50 per cent. Furthermore, only a small fraction of the native Americans were born on North Dakota soil, an

---

p. 107; *Co-operative Manager and Farmer*, IV (March, 1915), p. 21. The last publication, a supporter of Twitchell, described him as a resident of North Dakota "since the real cow boy days." Another publication charged that he came to Bismarck "to be the king bee of the progressive movement" but was defeated for speaker and went over to the opposition camp. *Industrial Freedom*, I (June, 1915), p. 19.

13. Richard Schmidt, "Leadership," *Encyclopaedia of the Social Sciences* (vols., New York, 1930–35), IX, 282–87.

14. Gaston, *The Nonpartisan League*, p. 45.

15. N. C. Abbott, "Social Center Development in North Dakota," University North Dakota, *Quarterly Journal*, II (July, 1912), p. 355.

scarcely any two families had come from the same part of the United States. The restlessness and change so characteristic of pioneer life had not been outgrown. A decade later, in 1920, it was reported that 86 per cent of the people of the state lived either on farms or in towns of less than 2,500. The 1920 census showed that, of a population of 648,872, some 515,009, or 79.6 per cent, were native-born and the remaining 131,863, or 20.4 per cent, were foreign-born. Of the latter, some 38,190 were born in Norway, 29,617 in Russia, 15,550 in Canada, 11,960 in Germany, and 10,453 in Sweden. The rest of the foreign population came from various parts of Europe.[16]

Townley was born in a region of northwestern Minnesota not unlike North Dakota. He attended the high school in Alexandria, Minnesota, and as a student he had become interested in debating and other forensic activities and had displayed an interest in religious, political, and economic issues. He taught school for a while but soon tired of the routine of the classroom and set out for the West in search of livelier pursuits.[17] His talent for organization first showed itself as he tried his luck at farming in the extreme western part of North Dakota near the Montana border, a submarginal farming area.[18] Since working with horses was too slow for him, he persuaded his neighbors to pool their resources and buy a steam tractor and plows. This was soon followed by other innovations, for he had always displayed impatience with doing things on a small scale. After forming a farming syndicate with neighbors, Townley withdrew when the prospects for a good crop looked slim and allowed the other members to divide the seed and equipment and take their chances. Heavy

16. *Statistical Abstract of the United States*, 1921, pp. 61, 73; *Fourteenth Census of the United States*, Vol. III, *Population*, 1920, p. 764.

17. Gaston, *The Nonpartisan League*, pp. 46–48.

18. Macy H. Lapham and Others, *Soil Survey of Western North Dakota*, U. S. Dept. Agri., Bureau of Soils (Washington, 1910), pp. 27–28. During the years 1892–1906 the acreage devoted to the production of wheat in North Dakota rose from 2,868,729 acres to 5,992,000 acres, with a total production in 1906 of nearly 8,000,000 bushels. The increased production was due mainly to agricultural expansion in western North Dakota. "In local districts and under unusually favorable conditions a yield of from 35 to 40 bushels per acre is sometimes harvested. The average yield is, however, much lighter, the average yield per acre for the State during the fifteen-year period cited above being 12.6 bushels. A yield of from 12 to 15 bushels per acre is usually considered profitable."

rains soon followed, however, and as a result those who had been associated with him prospered.

After spending a year wandering to the Pacific Coast, Townley returned
to North Dakota to try raising flax in the Golden Valley, where returns
from farming were very high.[19] During two fairly successful seasons, he
expanded his holdings beyond what might be termed sound economic
practice, and soon came to be known as the "flax king." Land agents
pointed him out as a successful farmer, but this reputation was short-lived:
his third farming year, 1912, proved disastrous. The payments on the additional land and machinery that he had purchased could not be made,
for the season was dry, the harvest small, and the prices low. Townley
himself attributed his failure to the speculators and the "grain gamblers,"
and disclaimed any responsibility on his part for his mishaps. This point
of view soon found its way into the "campaign of education" of the Nonpartisan League. Inefficient farm management and weather hazards as
causes for small crops, low prices, and small incomes had no place in
Townley's thinking. The farmer was not at all responsible for the conditions under which he farmed.

Townley's failure at farming drove him headlong into the Socialist
camp. North Dakota was a state fertile for the spreading of discontent and
the sowing of Socialist propaganda. Commercial wheat farming had
brought the farmer into direct relation with the organized grain trade,
financial institutions, the railroads, and the town merchants.[20] Agricultural
discontent was accentuated by the semiarid conditions prevailing in
large part of the state, for the farmers were not familiar with the existing
climatic hazards, or else they were indifferent to them and to the need of
diversified agriculture to insure some income regardless of weather conditions.[21] The Socialists capitalized on these conditions; they held meet-

19. Gaston, The Nonpartisan League, pp. 49–50.
20. James E. Le Rossignol, What is Socialism? (New York, 1921), pp. 239–4
Meyer Jacobstein, "The Aldrich Banking Plan," University of North Dako
Quarterly Journal, III (January, 1913), pp. 154–56.
21. Wheat farmers repeatedly were warned against the disastrous consequen
of single-crop farming. In 1889, for instance, Dakota farmers were advised: "Th
is money in gardening, in poultry and eggs, in butter and cheese, and a score of oth
things which seem trifling to a man who harvests 3,000 or 4,000 bushels of do
wheat, but supposing there is a hot wind, a lack of rain or a frost? The man w

ings, sold literature, and canvassed the farming areas for membership.[22]

The Socialist party of North Dakota was a fairly well organized unit from 1908 to 1914, despite the predominance of agricultural population in the state, and the party's influence was greater than its membership figures would indicate. As early as 1908 it had adopted a platform embodying the chief features of the Nonpartisan League, calling for state-owned elevators and mills, credit banks, and a system of state-owned and operated hail insurance. At Minot, a center of radical activities, the Socialists published the *Iconoclast*, which repeatedly urged the farmers to organize for political action.[23] It saw the American Society of Equity movement as a step in the direction of socialism but hardly sufficient to achieve the goal the Socialists desired. "We recognize the Equity as well as every other radical organization or movement, no matter what its name or label as a social force, and therefore a part of the great process of social evolution which will result in the eventual socialization of the na-

---

puts all his eggs in one basket is liable to go smash." Frank H. Hagerty, *The State of North Dakota, The Statistical, Historical and Political Abstract* (Aberdeen, S. Dak., 1889), p. 61.

The dairy commissioner's report for 1910 indicated that the failure to practice diversified farming in the state was not because of ignorance or indifference, but because of conditions that were difficult to overcome. The commissioner said, "When we consider the early settlement of this state at a time when it was possible to secure large tracts of land either by purchase at a nominal price, or through governmental regulations, and realize that the great majority of farmers have large farms, that diversified farming means building fences, barns, arranging for pastures and foods for live stock, that it calls for better and a higher grade of help, that it means more labor must be added to the farm, that there will be no months of leisure, and that the size of the farm practically prohibits their handling it in the most approved methods advocated by scientific agricultural experts, we realize more fully what it means for the grain farmer to take up diversified farming. It is not wholly prejudice, but a condition, that confronts them. . . ." *Biennial Report of the Dairy Commissioner to the Commissioner of Agriculture and Labor*, 1910, p. 8.

22. Arthur Le Sueur, "The Nonpartisan League" (unpublished manuscript in the Minnesota Historical Society), p. 2; *Iconoclast* (Minot, N. Dak.), July 17, 1914. Beecher Moore was a pioneer Socialist in North Dakota.

23. *Ibid*. See Frederick E. Haynes, *Social Politics in the United States* (Boston, 1921), pp. 204–8, for the distribution of political strength of the Socialists in the nation. Minot was the headquarters for the North Dakota Socialists. *State of North Dakota Legislative Manual*, 1913, pp. xxiii, 265–67. See also Le Sueur, "The Nonpartisan League," pp. 1–2.

tion's industries. It is the quintessence of jackassable stupidity to ignore any of the intermediate stages in the development of the social progress." [24] Experience soon pointed out that the Socialist program was more popular than the party itself, and quite appropriately so; the Farmers' Alliance had agitated for some of the same measures a couple of decades earlier.

In time the Socialists provided for an organization department within their party which made it possible for non-Socialists to join without having to sign "the red card of terrible reputation." The establishment of the department proved that the party itself did not appeal to the farmer but that its platform did. Socialist propaganda emphasized, among other things, that the farmer as an individual had certain duties to perform if he was to better himself; he had to learn to manage efficiently, to work diligently, to initiate state-owned mills and elevators, to launch cooperative associations, to practice diversified farming, and to use every other available opportunity to free himself from the "dominant" economic forces that ruled him. [25] The Socialist argument, in other words, placed some of the responsibility for the plight of the farmer on the farmer himself. This argument did not augur well for the welfare of the party. The farmer who attended a Socialist meeting and then went home to his tumbledown house, his uneducated children, his ragged, overworked wife, his weedy fields, and his rusty and outmoded machinery and then applied the doctrines he had heard would not have a comfortable feeling, for he could not escape from some measure of responsibility for his condition. [26]

24. *Iconoclast*, June 25, 1915.

25. Henry P. Richardson, "Scientific Organizing and the Farmer," *International Socialist Review*, XV (March, 1915), pp. 554–58, discusses Socialist organization problems among North Dakota farmers. The North Dakota Socialists used automobiles to contact farmers before the Nonpartisan League was organized.

26. In 1912 the Socialist party received 7.9 per cent of the state's total vote. It was surpassed by Oklahoma, Nevada, Montana, Washington, California, Idaho, Oregon, Florida, Arizona, Ohio, Wisconsin, Texas, Minnesota, and Utah in the order listed. The total Socialist vote in 1912 was 897,011, which was 5.9 per cent of the total national vote. In the presidential election of 1916, North Dakota was surpassed in Socialist strength by Oklahoma, Nevada, Florida, Wisconsin, Idaho, Washington, Arizona, Montana, and Texas. *The American Labor Yearbook*, 1917–18 (New York, 1918), pp. 336–37. In 1914 the membership of the Socialist party in Montana was 1,589; in North Dakota, 1,644; and in Minnesota, 4,965. In 1915 it was, respectively, 1,057 and 1,107 and 3,542. *Ibid.*, 1916, pp. 95–96. One source says: "Ameri-

In 1914 Townley volunteered to serve as an organizer for the organization department of the Socialist party to help test out the differences in popularity between the party and its platform. Supplied with plenty of Socialist literature and an automobile with which to travel from place to place, he held meetings arranged for him by headquarters, sold the literature, and took pledges from farmers who joined the organization department, not the Socialist party. When cash was not available, he accepted postdated checks.[27] Monthly dues of $1.00 were to be paid, and the platform and the candidates of the organization were to be supported.

Townley's success was almost instantaneous. In less than three months he had four organizers at work—men who, it was claimed, were members of the Socialist party. There is still a difference of opinion, however, on whether Townley himself was actually a member. The expenses of the organizers were paid from the receipts for the literature, from contributions, and from the thousands of pledges received. But this experiment, was short-lived, for at the Socialist convention in 1915 the state committee recommended the discontinuance of the work of the organization department. The committee charged that such a program was inconsistent with the future welfare of the party and the farmers and pointed out that the organization department had as many members as did the party itself, the main difference being that the members of the latter were educated on the subject of socialism, while those of the former were not.

When the Socialist party refused to permit Townley to continue organizing, he felt that he had been poorly treated. Consequently, when A. E. Bowen, an associate, recommended that they organize a nonpartisan organization having nothing to do with the Socialist party, Townley was immediately impressed with the idea.[28] Townley and Bowen were both

---

can Socialism seems . . . to have its chief strength, not in the manufacturing centers, but in those Western states where mining and farm tenantry prevail." *Ibid.*, 1917–18, p. 338.

27. Le Sueur, "The Nonpartisan League," p. 4; J. D. Bacon, *A Warning to the Farmer against Townleyism as Exploited in North Dakota* (Grand Forks, N. Dak., 1918), p. 11.

28. Le Sueur, "The Nonpartisan League," p. 5; *Milwaukee Leader,* July 29, 1916. One Socialist leader charged: "The Socialist organization of North Dakota is today a travesty and a farce. The red-card organizers of the league are yet 'comrades' and control the Socialist Party."

credited with being the "midwives" of the Nonpartisan League, and although the statement to the effect that Townley stole the Nonpartisan idea from Bowen frequently circulated, it was the organizing genius of Townley that placed the new organization on its feet.[29]

Political action appeared feasible to the farmers at the time because it held out promises that were not to be achieved readily by other, slower means. Besides, the rate at which North Dakota farmers were joining the organization department of the Socialist party indicated that a new movement was on foot; all that was needed was the leadership. The grievances of the farmers against the organized grain trade were well known, and the psychological moment for the new movement had already presented itself.

Organization of the Nonpartisan League began shortly after the memorable Equity meeting of February, 1915. At this convention Townley renewed his acquaintanceship with F. B. Wood, a highly respected and admired Equity leader whom he had met in the course of his work for the Socialist party. Conversations between the two shortly followed, and Wood later admitted that he "had told Townley that he could come to our farm when spring broke and I would help him get started." Townley, however, could not wait until spring, and the two talked the matter over again. This time Wood's two sons sat in; and the following morning Townley and Howard Wood, one of the sons, "started out with a team and bobsled to call on the neighbors. The Farmers' Nonpartisan Political League of North Dakota had begun organizations. . . . Howard Wood furnished the introductions. Townley did the talking. It was an arrangement that later became a standard of methods in League organization work." Howard Wood, the convert, became the "booster" in the township, accompanying the organizer to "break the ice with his neighbors." The League reportedly enrolled twelve members the first day.[30]

Soon the Ford car was introduced into the League's organizing operations in order to cover wider stretches of territory. That Townley was preparing to deal the state a political blitzkrieg in a day when such terminology was unknown soon became apparent. Organizers and members

29. S. R. Maxwell, *The Nonpartisan League from the Inside* (St. Paul, 1918), p. 44.

30. Gaston, *The Nonpartisan League*, pp. 56–58.

were cautioned to keep their membership confidential, "to keep all knowledge of the movement from the leeches who sucked their blood," and the work proceeded without organized opposition.[31] One newspaper was quoted as saying:

It is being rumored . . . that a number of strange characters are operating in this part . . . whose business is not definitely known. It is claimed, however, by those who profess to know, that they are organizing a farmers' political league of some kind or other. They go about in Ford cars, leaving town early in the morning and returning late at night. They tell no one their business voluntarily and when the question is put directly to them, reply that they are selling washing machines. It is needless to say that the farmers of this community are too intelligent and prosperous to be taken in by any wild-eyed scheme of a political nature and certainly if they want washing machines our enterprising merchants have plenty of them to sell. If, however, farmers are approached or pestered on any new proposition which they do not understand thoroughly, we urge them not to sign any papers or make any pledges or promises until after they have consulted with their banker or with the editor of this paper. Beware of gold-brick agents.[32]

The methods employed in organizing the League represented a curious blend of socialism and high-pressure salesmanship. Farmers were advised to do as "big business" did when it came to organizing for politics. League leaders pointed out that "big business" was "absolutely nonpartisan and well-financed; it operated politically through the dominant parties or in any other way that comes in handy." They cited the case of Jay Gould, who, when asked what his politics were, replied, "In Democratic states I am a Democrat; in Republican states I am a Republican, but I am always for the Erie Railway." [33]

The League propaganda was "intended to shock and startle and stir up" both the reader and the listener and represented "the farmer as an upright and down-trodden member of society and Big Business as the vil-

31. [James Frost], Townley & Co. and the Nonpartisan League (Beach, N. Dak., 1918), p. 31. See also J. W. Brinton, Wheat and Politics (Minneapolis, 1931), pp. 36–37.

32. O. M. Thomason, The Beginning and the End of the Nonpartisan League (n.p., 1920), pp. 105–6.

33. As quoted in Nonpartisan League Methods and Principles (Waco, Texas, n.d.), p. 10 [booklet].

lain."[34] Arguments were advanced to substantiate reasons why the farmers should control the political life of North Dakota. To a degree, they resembled those of the French physiocrats, who strongly upheld the superiority of agriculture over other forms of economic activity. League leaders pointed to agriculture as the basic industry, "the most important industry under the shining sun. Emperors, Kings, Ministers, Presidents, Parliaments, Congresses, great generals, mighty armies with monster guns and forests of bayonets and mountains of shot and shell, are down on their knees before the man with the hoe. Yet, he has had but little direct voice in affairs of government that determine his weal or woe. Men who can hardly tell the difference between a cotton boll and a chrysanthemum, are expected to legislate for the most vital industry of all. . . ." The League demanded "proportional occupational representation" as a means of eliminating the imposter from public life. It was maintained that a representative of the farmers, with a knowledge of the views of that economic group, would be more likely to legislate in accordance with the needs of the farmers than one representing a variety of economic interests. It was not "sleek, smooth-tongued, bay-windowed fellows that looked well, talked well, lived well, lied well" who could best run the government. The case of the North Dakota farmers was but one instance where "the farmers had been vainly begging a bunch of wind-jamming, poker-playing, booze-fighting politicians for legislation to protect them against the flour-mill trust and the grain gamblers. . . ." If the farmers of North Dakota constituted 83 per cent of the population, they said, why should they not "control 83 per cent of the government." [35]

Greater confidence was obtained among the farmers by limiting the organization to actual tillers of the soil and later by encouraging practical cooperation with organized labor. Office seekers were to be eliminated by nominating as candidates for public office a farmer, a wage earner, or anyone else "tried in the field of unselfish service." Campaign expenses were to be financed with fees that were high enough to cover the costs, the candidates in turn being tied to the farmer organization in the same manner that the candidate from big business was tied to the business interests.

34. John M. Gillette, "The North Dakota Harvest of the Nonpartisan League," *Survey*, XLI (March 1, 1919), pp. 759–60.

35. *Nonpartisan League Methods and Principles*, pp. 14–15.

That the actual administration of the League would be highly centralized was accepted as axiomatic almost from the very beginning. It was dominated by a committee of three that was democratic in form but despotic in practice.[36] Townley was chairman of the committee, the other two members being William Lemke and F. B. Wood. Tenure on this committee was indefinite since there was no provision for the election of successors. The opposition made much of this centralized control, but Townley's replies placated the rank and file, temporarily at least, and typified his ability to obtain their confidence. "Are not the milling interests organized and ably led by a few men?" he asked. "And the interests that manufacture agricultural machinery? And the railroads? Does anybody know of a single great interest in this country that is not highly organized?"[37]

The actual organizing of the farmers was one of the most dramatic aspects of the League, for it had gathered together one of the most artful groups of radical writers and speakers the nation had ever seen. They were thoroughly saturated with radical doctrines, techniques of indoctrination, and large-scale organization methods. In knowledge of mass psychology they were unsurpassed. They were capable of finding the least common denominator among their farmer listeners; they adopted few themes, and they repeated them untiringly. Townley, in particular, was a man of striking physical appearance, boisterous in talk but rich in expression; and the League leaders in general were capable of pointing out the enemy to the farmers in simple fashion. In North Dakota the League encountered no difficulty in arousing the farmers against their traditional foes—the railroads, the financial interests, and the press. League leaders ably fed the passions of the farmers by telling them exactly what they wanted to hear.

In contacting the farmers the League's organizers were instructed to ascertain the particular interests of the farmer and to talk about them instead of necessarily the League program, to agree with everything the farmer said, and to condemn everything he disliked. This approach is epitomized in a former League leader's account of Townley's instructions.

36. *Nonpartisan League; Origin, Purpose and Method of Operation, War Program and Statement of Principles* (n.p., n.d.), pp. 10-11; James Manahan, *Trials of a Lawyer* (Minneapolis, 1933), p. 221.

37. *Why Should Farmers Pay Dues?* (St. Paul, n.d.), p. 7 [booklet].

"Make the rubes pay their god-damn money to join and they'll stick—stick 'til hell freezes over." Organizers were drilled on how to "organize" the farmer in his barn yard; how to "surround the rube," one man in front and one on each side, facing him, and all urging him to join. . . . "Find out the damn fool's hobby," taught Townley, "and then talk it. If he likes religion, talk Jesus Christ; if he is against the government, damn the democrats; if he is afraid of whiskey, preach prohibition; if he wants to talk hogs, talk hogs—talk anything he'll listen to, but talk, talk, until you get his god-damn John Hancock to a check for six dollars."[38]

In short, the tricks of the accomplished salesman and the orator were put into full swing by an ably trained group of radicals advocating a Socialist program. Many of the grievances they aired were no doubt highly exaggerated, but they achieved the desired end of increasing membership. In many rural areas strong appeals were made to the antipathies of farmers toward town merchants and business interests. Even national feeling and racial pride were used; organizers were instructed "to put a soft pedal on all the Wilson stuff" when organizing in German communities.[39] Mass meetings and large picnics were arranged to supplement the work of the organizers and sometimes to pave the way for them in new territory. Whether League organizers approached the farmer in his barn or whether they addressed him in public meetings, the expression "Go home and slop the hogs" was used with increasing effectiveness.

A potent factor in the early successes of the League was the Nonpartisan League press, which, according to one writer, furnished "a significant case study in the use of propaganda by a highly class-conscious pressure group." Nowhere within the organization, with the possible exception of the speaker's platform, were the gifts of expression better demonstrated than in the columns of the League press.[40] League writers warned the members not to trust the existing press; they were skilled in the techniques of indoctrination, and "with astute realism they anticipate[d] a wave of opposition from newspapers within and without the state. . . ." Charles Edward Russell, the noted Socialist publicist and editor of the *Non-partisan Leader,* the official organ, warned against "tainted news,"

38. Manahan, *Trials of a Lawyer,* pp. 219–20.

39. Maxwell, *The Nonpartisan League from the Inside,* pp. 82–85.

40. Joseph H. Mader, "The North Dakota Press and the Nonpartisan League," *Journalism Quarterly,* XIV (December, 1937), pp. 321–23.

"poisonous news," and the "poisoned special article." An early issue of the *Non-partisan Leader* cautioned: "The greatest advantage the interests and corporations have is their control over the press. That is where the first great danger lies before your organization. Beware of it; it is the greatest power in the world, the most subtle, insidious, poisonous, the hardest to detect and the hardest to defeat." [41] When the opposition press unleashed its attack upon the League, the skill and ingenuity of its journalists were well demonstrated in the retaliatory tactics. Little time was lost in portraying big business as the mortal enemy of the farmer in both cartoons and articles.[42] Feature articles were written in praise of government ownership, particularly in Australia and New Zealand. Editorials were written simply; they were graphic and presented to attract attention. Cartoons generally carried the point across.[43]

The organization work was in high gear by the close of 1915, and it is estimated that the League conducted five to six hundred meetings during the winter of 1915-16. By February, 1917, some 30,000 members were reported enrolled, and about three-fourths of the state was organized.[44] Shortly after the organization work of 1915, preparations were made for the 1916 election by calling precinct meetings to assemble on February 22, 1916, and elect delegates to a state convention.[45] These meetings were to be held at the regular polling places in each precinct, unless other arrangements already had been made. Parallels were drawn between the acts of the North Dakota farmers of February, 1916, and the American Revolution of 1776. "The conditions under which the people . . . in 1776 suffered . . . are only unlike in degree to the present conditions which the farmers are suffering in North Dakota." [46]

The meetings were well attended in each of the 2,000 precincts of North Dakota, and delegates were elected to legislative and district conventions.[47] The district conventions nominated candidates for both houses of

41. *Non-partisan Leader,* September 23, 1915, p. 7; October 21, 1915, p. 4.
42. F. A. Teigen, *The Nonpartisan League* (St. Paul, 1918), p. 45.
43. Gillette, in *Survey,* XLI (March, 1919), pp. 759-60.
44. *Literary Digest,* LIV (January 20, 1917), p. 115.
45. *Non-partisan Leader,* January 27, 1916, p. 5.
46. *Ibid.,* February 10, 1916, p. 6.
47. *Literary Digest,* LIV (January 20, 1917), p. 115; *Non-partisan Leader,* March 2, 1916, p. 3.

the legislature and delegates to a state convention which met at Fargo on March 29 and 30. The League candidates were as follows: for governor, Lynn J. Frazier of Hoople, graduate of the University of North Dakota, to run in the Republican primary; for lieutenant-governor, Albert Stenmo of Merrifield, Grand Forks County, graduate of the University of North Dakota, to run in the Republican primary; for secretary of state, Thomas Hall, the incumbent, to run as a Republican; for auditor, Carl R. Kositsky of Bismarck, secretary of the state tax commission and a Burleigh County commissioner, to run as a Republican; for treasurer, P. M. Casey, vice-president of the North Dakota Society of Equity, to run as a Democrat; for attorney-general, William A. Langer of Mandan, state attorney for Morton County, to run as a Republican; for superintendent of public instruction, N. C. MacDonald of Valley City, graduate of the University of North Dakota and state inspector of consolidated schools, to run on the nonpartisan school ballot; for commissioner of insurance, S. A. Olsness, a farmer at Cheyenne in Eddy County, to run as a Republican; for commissioner of agriculture, John Hagan of Deering in McHenry County, a graduate of Valparaiso University in Indiana, town supervisor for eleven years and a farmer, running on the Republican ticket. Candidates for railroad commissioners were Charles Bleick of Elgin, Morton County, an active Equity and Farmers' Union man and a graduate of the Nebraska School of Agriculture; M. P. Johnson of Tolley, Renville County, president of the North Dakota Society of Equity; and Sam Aandal, a farmer from Litchville, Barnes County—all running on the Republican ticket. Those running for the bench of the supreme court were Luther Birdzell, former state tax commissioner and professor of law in the University of North Dakota; J. E. Robinson, a Fargo lawyer; and R. H. Grace, lawyer from Mohall—all three running on the nonpartisan ballot in the primaries.[48]

As announced, League officials and organizers were not permitted to accept a nomination for state office, the theory being that the office should seek the man and not the man the office.[49] Furthermore, only farmer members had seats in the convention in which candidates for posts ranging from representatives in the state legislature to governor were endorsed. County politics were of no concern to the League.

48. *Ibid.*, April 6, 1916, p. 3.
49. *Nonpartisan League Methods and Principles*, p. 12.

The nomination of Lynn Frazier for governor represented an ingenious piece of politics, for, according to his sponsors, he was "a plain farmer, with no political record which they could misrepresent." [50] At the time of his nomination Frazier was forty-one years old. He was a native American and a farmer—"not an imitation farmer nor a town farmer, either," for he worked the land his father had been farming since 1881. Frazier, like Townley, was born in Minnesota, his parents moving to Pembina County, Dakota Territory, in 1881. There the father built a sod house, and when Frazier graduated from high school at the age of seventeen, he and his brother took up the task of running the farm, their father having died the previous year. Having developed an ambition to become a professional man, Frazier taught school for two years and saved enough money to enter the Mayville Normal School. He completed his course in one year, graduating in 1895 with the school's first class. After teaching school for another two years, Frazier entered the University of North Dakota at Grand Forks. There he displayed qualities as a student and an athlete, his main sport being football. Frazier was the "square blocky type, ideal for a center in those days of driving line rushes." He was football captain for two years and graduated in 1901 with a good scholastic record and many honors bestowed upon him by his classmates. Meanwhile, the brother in charge of the family farm had died, and consequently Frazier had to give up all ideas of a profession and return to the "prosaic work of being a farmer." [51]

If Townley and Lemke were unaware of the wisdom of their choice of Frazier as the "political pontiff" of the League, they were soon convinced of it. Upon his nomination Frazier was immediately labeled the "modern Cincinnatus" who was "called from the plow to head his people and to govern a great commonwealth." [52] He was "blessed by the substantial figure and confident pose of a statesman. He looked like a bishop. But Farmer Frazier was at that time untrained and inexperienced as a public speaker." Townley and Lemke then assigned him the job of meeting the farmers and selling himself with his "wholesomeness and unassumed solidity." Public meetings were widely advertised and usually

50. *Where the People Rule* (n.p., n.d.), p. 6 [pamphlet].
51. *Non-partisan Leader*, April 6, 1916, pp. 3, 5, 6.
52. *Ibid.*, April 27, 1916, p. 7.

held out of doors. Farmers drove miles to hear him. "He stood before them, sunburned and baldheaded. His voice was firm and persuasive. He spoke briefly and the tired farmers loved him." [53]

Townley and other League leaders emphasized the need for victory in the primary election by painting lurid pictures of the consequences that would follow the defeat of League candidates:

> If the farmers and their friends lose . . . North Dakota will be drained to the limit of her ability to pay. Homesteads will be mortgaged and lost. As in the past, horses, machinery and household goods will be sold under the hammer and the tillers of the soil will be turned out of their homes. Merchants will go broke because the farmers can not pay their store bill. Heavy mortgages, high interest, low prices, will force long hours of toil. Wives, mothers and sisters will work in the field. Children will be kept out of school summers to plow, seed and harvest, and kept at home winters for lack of money to pay the way through high school or college. All will be debt and drudgery. Mothers and fathers will die from overwork and worry while yet they should be young.
>
> Meanwhile we will yield up tens of millions of the earnings of our wives and daughters and mothers and fathers and brothers to the greedy masters of trade and finance in the East—millions that they do not need and can not use—millions that should be spent in North Dakota to make happy and prosperous a great people in a great state—millions that should be spent by North Dakota farmers with North Dakota business men to the greater advantage of both. All this—as in the past—*if we lose*.[54]

Frazier, despite his lack of political experience, displayed all the earmarks of one willing to learn; furthermore, there was something appealing about his inexperienced campaigning. "Public speaking like this is out of my line, I must admit," he said. "I am not a politician, but I can milk and slop hogs and fill the bill on the farm." [55] "[When told that] I was chosen to lead the farmers' ticket to victory, I thought that they had made a mistake." This approach appealed to the farmers, and the *Nonpartisan Leader* made much capital of the fact that his speeches were "unadorned with flourishes."

A novelty of the campaign that caused amazement among the experienced politicians was the chartering of a special train, the "Frazier

53. Manahan, *Trials of a Lawyer*, pp. 221–22.
54. *Non-partisan Leader*, June 1, 1916, p. 1.
55. *Ibid.*, April 13, 1916, p. 16.

Special." This type of campaigning was not, however, the invention of the Nonpartisan League. In 1908 the Socialist presidential candidate, Eugene V. Debs, was carried to all parts of the country in the "Red Special." [56] The chances are that the League leaders borrowed this idea from the Socialist party, whence many of them had come. The "Frazier Special" was scheduled to stop at all important points in North Dakota during the last week of the campaign, which closed on June 28, primary day. [57] It carried the League candidates and it was intended to give the farmers a chance to hear the case of the farmers. A series of picnics were arranged with five-, ten-, and fifteen-minute speeches by the candidate for governor and his party. An opportunity was also given the prospective voters to board the "Frazier Special" and ride from their home station to the nearest mass meeting by simply purchasing a ticket. Business offices, stores, and shops were closed in honor of the occasion in some of the towns, including New Rockford, Jamestown, Valley City, Bottineau, and Minot. [58]

Frazier, running true to form, defeated four candidates in the primaries and received a larger vote than the opposition candidates combined. [59] In fact, the League "swirled" into the campaign and "tore it wide open." All its candidates were nominated on the Republican ticket with the exception of P. M. Casey, its choice for treasurer "whom the Democrats obligingly nominated." [60] A Mandan newspaper, upon hearing of the nomination of Frazier, asked: "Who in Hell is Frazier, and Where in Hell is Hoople?" [61] As a result of the League showing, both the Republican and Democratic parties adopted programs largely in accord with the League platform. [62]

Originally, the League had announced that it would support only candidates for the state executive, judiciary, and legislative offices, but it di-

56. Haynes, *Social Politics in the United States,* pp. 196–97; McAlister Coleman, *Eugene V. Debs* (New York, 1930), pp. 244–48; David Karsner, *Debs* (New York, 1919), pp. 190–91.
57. *Non-partisan Leader,* June 15, 1916, p. 8.
58. *Ibid.,* July 6, 1916, p. 5.
59. Brinton, *Wheat and Politics,* p. 37.
60. *Literary Digest,* LIV (January 20, 1917), p. 115.
61. Brinton, *Wheat and Politics,* p. 37.
62. *Non-partisan Leader,* November 30, 1916, p. 5.

verted sufficiently to support Porter McCumber for re-election to the United States Senate. Officially, the League endorsed no candidates for county offices or for the Presidency; secretly, according to report, it endorsed Woodrow Wilson, although Lynn Frazier was for Charles Evans Hughes.[63]

In the November election the League again achieved a thunderous victory by capturing every elective state office but one and electing three justices who had endorsed the League program for state-owned utilities to the supreme court.[64] Of the 107,000 votes cast, Frazier received 87,000, or 80 per cent.[65] The farmers, however, forgot to "remember Casey," the League candidate for treasurer, who ran on the Democratic ticket. The League gained control of every branch of the government except the senate, the majority in the house being 85 per cent. North Dakota presented the anomalous situation of having elected a Republican governor over the Democratic candidate by a vote of four to one and a Republican senator over a Democrat by an overwhelming majority and yet having given the Democratic presidential candidate a safe majority.[66]

The postelection comments were amusing. Nonpartisan leaders pronounced the results as the beginning of "a peaceful revolution" that had "found its place of incubation in the Northwest states."[67] One correspondent pointed out that "ten months ago Governor Frazier was unknown outside of his own precinct," and another queried whether "slopping hogs is the right sort of training for anyone charged with the grave duties of state's chief executive." The wonder of the election was that the League had "dipt into its first political campaign," before it was a year old; "even more astonishing" were the results when one considers North Dakota's "magnificent distances." Well over 80 per cent of its population was scattered on farms that could be reached for the most part only by a personal canvass.[68]

63. *The New International Year Book*, 1916, p. 496; *Non-partisan Leader*, November 2, 1916, p. 8.

64. *Literary Digest*, LIV (January 20, 1917), p. 115.

65. *Non-partisan Leader*, January 18, 1917, p. 7.

66. *Ibid.*, November 16, 1916, p. 3; *Literary Digest*, LIV (January 20, 1917) p. 115; *The New International Year Book*, 1916, p. 496.

67. *Non-partisan Leader*, February 22, 1917, p. 3.

68. *Ibid.*, January 4, 1917, p. 2; *Literary Digest*, LIV (January 20, 1917), p. 115